VOICES OF THE VALLEY

VOICES OF THE VALLEY

AN ANTHOLOGY OF CORVALLIS POETS

Steven Sher & Michael Spring
Editors

Linda Varsell Smith
Corvallis Consulting Editor

Flowstone Press

Voices of the Valley: An Anthology of Corvallis Poets
Copyright © 2026 Steven Sher and Michael Spring
Linda Varsell Smith, Corvallis consulting editor

First Flowstone Press edition January 2026
ISBN-13: 978-1-945824-67-8

These poems are reprinted by permission of the poets.
Barbara Baldwin's poems by permission of
CALYX Books and Rachel Baldwin.
Richard Dankleff's poems by permission of Oregon State University Press.
Be Davison Herrera's poems by permission of Betu Herrera Case.
Peter Sears's poems by permission of Anita Helle,
the Estate of Peter Sears and Small Talk.
Susan Spady's poems by permission of Beth Littlehales and Emily Spady.
Peggy Taylor's poems by permission of
University of Oregon Knight Library Special Collections.
Dale Willey's poems by permission of Dave Willey.
CALYX covers by permission of CALYX Books.
Photo editing by N. Sher.

Flowstone Press,
an imprint of Left Fork
Illinois Valley, Oregon

for
Michael Spring,
who created enduring poetry
and community. May all he touched
be blessed by his memory and good name.

Contents

Ephemera — xii
Introduction — 3

Chris Anderson — 8
The Soft Allegorical Woods — 10
Paper Maple — 11
The Neskowin Cottage Walk — 11
Our Trip to Spokane for a Wedding — 12
We Who Move — 13

Sara Backer — 14
Such Luck — 16
Jack — 17
The Drowning Man — 18
Your Egret — 19
Leaving the City Behind — 20

Barbara Baldwin — 22
Aubade — 24
For My Sister — 24
Bessie — 25
Huérfano — 26
August 1948 — 27

Rachel Barton — 28
If the Orange Cones Were Pawns I Would Be Queen — 30
A Far Cry — 31
Slow Crossing — 32
Cameras in His Closet — 33
Stepping into the Wild — 34

David Biespiel — 36
Room — 38
The Theory of Hats — 39
A Man Feels the World — 40
Though Your Sins Be Scarlet — 41
With Passing Wonder I Notice the Tracks of an Animal — 42

Dorothy Black Crow	44
Songs to the Sea	46
Wave after Wave, Sea-Breathing	48
Whatever Grows in Salt Air	49
Hold Fast	50
Believe in the Ocean	51
Richard Dankleff	52
Flute Song	54
Adah	54
Lt. Montgomery Pike Harrison	55
When the Stars Fell	56
Grasshopper Summer	57
Greg Darling	58
Fire and Ice	60
Immigrant	60
Truck	61
A Ponderance	62
Letter to Celeste from the Great North Woods	63
Eric Wayne Dickey	64
Upon Watching a Reenactment of a Civil War Battle	66
Pretzel Legs	66
After You Left	67
James Dean	68
Face on the Floor	69
George Estreich	70
Written in the Air	72
Daughter, 4, Traces Newspaper	72
Codes	76
Reasons for Building	82
Linda Gelbrich	84
Watching a Wasp the Day after John Lewis's Funeral	86
Summer Sounds in the Neighborhood	87
Brittle	87
Along a Trail at Shotpouch Creek	88
Listen to the River	89

Charles Goodrich — 90
- A Lecture on Aphids — 92
- Vacuuming Spiders — 93
- Why We Do It — 94
- Interstition — 96
- Wild Geese — 96

Donna Henderson — 98
- Transparent Woman — 100
- Lunar — 102
- First Ice — 103
- Between Sleeping and Waking — 104
- The Sanctuary — 105

Be Davison Herrera — 108
- A Blues Song — 110
- I Might Enjoy Being Wordless — 110
- Meditations on the Song Celestial — 111
- Talk to Me … I will Listen — 112
- Cold Food Day — 113

Karen Holmberg — 114
- The Slug — 116
- Exchange of Azalea and Quail — 117
- To the Ox Netsuke in the Flea Market — 118
- Surrogate — 119
- Sweetbriar — 121

Steve Jones — 122
- Next There's Fish — 124
- Twilight Golf — 124
- Traveling the Circle of Twenty Apes — 125
- When People Turned to Pebbles — 126
- Old Tools — 127

Michael Malan — 128
- The Moving House — 130
- A New Language — 130
- A Really Good Smoke — 131
- My Brother Running — 132
- My Father's House — 133

Jennifer Richter	134
Threshold:	136
She Asks about Death, Then Draws	136
Recovery 6: The Last Word	137
My Daughter Brings Home Bones	137
Love Poem Grounded in the Seismic Communication of Elephants	138
Lex Runciman	140
One Thing	142
Applause	143
Overlook House	144
Beach Agates	145
The Waiting	146
Peter Sears	148
Snow at Night	150
Traffic Jam on the Ross Island Bridge	150
American Hero: A Poem Made into a Movie	151
Bummer	152
Who's the Who Walking Beside Me?	153
Matthew Shenoda	154
Somewhere Else	156
Where We Come From	157
Reclaiming the Classroom (after Three for Phil McGee)	159
Al-Mansūra (Nile Blues)	161
Dispatches from the New World Order	162
Steven Sher	164
The Skipping Stone	166
Secrets	167
The Man Who Brought His Own Food	167
The House of Washing Hands	168
Revealing What Is Hidden	169
Linda Varsell Smith	170
Demidonne in an Antique Shop	172
The Sand Spider	173
Hallowing Ground	174
The Land Octopus	175
Shifting Attention	177

Susan Spady — 178
- Carrying Eggs — 180
- Rock Paper Scissors — 181
- Pot-Pot-Pots — 182
- Underpants — 183
- Pretending — 184

Michael Spring — 186
- indecision — 188
- the woman Miles Davis turned down — 189
- beneath a plum tree — 190
- fishing with my son — 191
- what kind of fish can survive this river — 192

Ann Staley — 194
- Afternoon Sky, Harney Desert — 196
- Upwelling — 197
- Rhymes with Dammit — 197
- November Ghazal — 198
- Clouded Nights — 199

Clemens Starck — 200
- A Lesson in Physics — 202
- Journeyman's Wages — 202
- Dismantling — 203
- Deciding the Course My Education Should Take — 204
- Job No. 75–14 — 206

Doug Stone — 208
- The Wilson River Road — 210
- Spring Arrives in the Hoh Rain Forest — 210
- Letter from Oregon — 211
- Requiem for Celilo Falls — 211
- Somewhere between Bend and Boise — 212

Anita Sullivan — 214
- Wool Light — 216
- Willamette-ites — 216
- Green — 217
- Owl Dialogue — 218
- The Day Arrives — 219

Peggy Taylor — 220
- Fairie Tail — 222
- Brigid — 222
- Walking the Dog — 223
- I Can … — 224
- To My Lover's Legs — 225

Roger Weaver — 226
- Build Down — 228
- What the Azaleas Didn't Say — 228
- Patterns — 228
- Fir Trees — 229
- Skating up the Sky — 229

Dale Willey — 230
- Ionesco's Theme — 232
- I Could Eat You Up — 233
- The Old Woods — 234
- Nightfall — 235
- The Sinuous — 236

EPHEMERA

Benton County Writers Centennial Bookmark 1999	1
The Magic Barrel : A Reading to Fight Hunger, Majestic Theatre 2004; da Vinci Days program 1997	2
CALYX Vol 1:1; *CALYX* Vol 29:2	21
Westerns, Oregon State University Press 1984; *From Here We Speak: An Anthology of Oregon Poetry*, OSU Press 1993	35
Artspirit Jan/Feb 1998; Diverse Voices: Willamette Literary Guild Cross-Cultural Readings 1994	43
Words of Healing Worlds of Hope; World AIDS Day 2002; Poetic License reading 2006	83
Marys Peak Sentinel of the Coast Range photography and poetry 2001; *Tcha teemanwi: Poems for Marys Peak* 2001	97
Mistry Guild Vol 1 1999; *Fireweed* Vol 6:2 winter 1995	107
Midway Theatre marquees	139
Arrowood Books titles	147
Poets of Faith reading 2001; Literary Cabaret, Corvallis Arts Center 1992	163
Let Us Drink to the River 1997; *River Songs from the Willamette River Diptych* 1999; *Riven* 1 2003	185
Midway Theatre marquee; Ekphrasis: Poets Ponder Photographs 2010	207
To Topio 1997; *To Topus* 2003	213
The Eloquent Umbrella 1990; *The Eloquent Umbrella* 1998	237
Cloudbank Books reading, Grass Roots Books & Music 2004; Valley Writers Series, Linn-Benton Community College 1991–92	238

Right in Our Own Back Yard

BENTON COUNTY WRITERS

A SAMPLING of the work of Benton County writers—past and present—in your library!

1899 to 1999 - 100 Years of Great Reading!

FICTION
- 1904 Dennis Stovall. *Suzanne of Kerbyville.* STOVALL, DENNIS FICTION
- 1961 Bernard Malamud. *A New Life.* MALAMUD, BERNARD FICTION
- 1986 Rick Borsten. *The Great Equalizer.* BORSTEN, RICK FICTION
- 1994 Patricia Rowe. *Keepers of the Misty Time.* ROWE, PATRICIA FICTION
- 1996 Tracy Daugherty. *What Falls Away: A Novel.* DAUGHER, TRACY FICTION
- 1996 Gregg Kleiner. *Where River Turns to Sky.* KLEINER, GREGG FICTION
- 1998 Ehud Havazelet. *Like Never Before.* HAVAZELET, EHUD FICTION

NON-FICTION
- 1900 Louis Albert Banks. *Live Boys in Oregon, or An Oregon Boyhood.* 979.5 BANKS
- 1916 Louise G. Stephens. *From an Oregon Ranch, by "Katherine."* 979.5 STEPHENS
- 1931 John B. Horner. *Oregon History and Early Literature: A Pictorial Narrative of the Pacific Northwest.* 979.5 HORNER
- 1951 Helen Margaret Gilkey & Garland M. Powell. *Handbook of Northwest Flowering Plants.* 582.13 GILKEY
- 1964 Edwin R. Jackman. *The Oregon Desert.* 917.95 JACKMAN

A Centennial Bookmark
Sponsored by Zonta Club of Corvallis

- 1967 William Hugh Carlson. *In a Grand and Awful Time: Essays from the Librarian's Desk on Twentieth-Century Man and His Books.* 814 CARLSON
- 1969 Ava Milam Clark & J. Kenneth Munford. *Adventures of a Home Economist.* 921 CLARK
- 1985 Anita T. Sullivan. *The Seventh Dragon: The Riddle of Equal Temperament.* 781.23 SULLIVAN
- 1990 Jan Roberts-Dominguez. *Sandwich Cuisine: Oregon Style.* 641.8409 ROBERTS
- 1992 Helen Ashton Tedder & Marlene Johnson. *The Buddy Diet: How Two of You Can Keep It Off Together.* 613.7 TEDDER
- 1998 Jeff Damon Taylor. *Tools of the Earth: The Practice and Pleasure of Gardening.* 635.9134 TAYLOR
- 1998 Wendy Madar. *Through Another Lens: My Years with Edward Weston.* 770.92 WILSON

POETRY
- 1957 *A Century of Benton County Poetry: A Collection of Original Poetry by Benton County Poets.* 810.8 CENTURY
- 1977 Gary Lark. *Eels and Fishes.* 811.54 LARK
- 1978 Roger Weaver. *The Orange: And Other Poems.* 811.54 WEAVER
- 1985 Richard N. Matzen. *Behind Signs: A Blue Beat Poetic Zen Letter from Leo Curzen.* 811.54 MATZEN
- 1989 Lex Runciman. *The Admirations: Poems.* 811.54 RUNCIMAN
- 1994 Steven Sher. *Traveler's Advisory: Poems.* 811.54 SHER

ESPECIALLY FOR THE YOUNG
- 1982 Anne Warren Smith. *Blue Denim Blues.* J SMITH, ANNE FICTION
- 1989 Linda Crew. *Children of the River.* J CREW, LINDA FICTION
- 1994 Tom Birdseye. *A Regular Flood of Mishap.* E BIRDSEY, TOM
- 1997 Margaret J. Anderson. *Children of Summer: Henri Fabre's Insects.* J ANDERSON, MARGARET FICTION

Corvallis-Benton County Public Library
"Bringing People and Information Together"

the magic barrel
a reading to fight hunger

Carol Ann Bassett
Tom Birdseye
Alison Clement
George Estreich
Jennifer Richter
Keith Scribner
Richard Dankleff, read by Clem Starck
Jana Zvibleman

Jazz by the Xtet

Majestic Theater
Friday, November 19, 2004 ~ 7pm

~ sponsored in part by the OSU Center for the Humanities ~

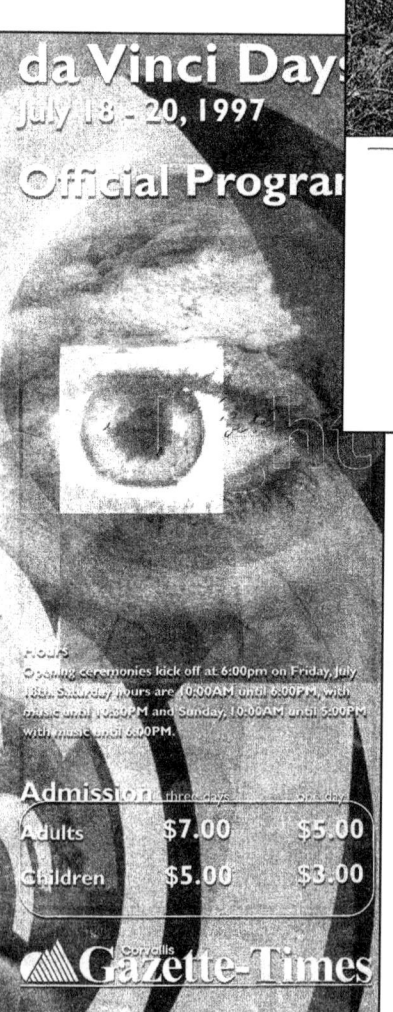

da Vinci Days
July 18 - 20, 1997
Official Program

Hours
Opening ceremonies kick off at 6:00pm on Friday, July 18th. Saturday hours are 10:00AM until 6:00PM, with music until 10:30PM and Sunday, 10:00AM until 5:00PM with music until 6:00PM.

Admission three days / one day

	three days	one day
Adults	$7.00	$5.00
Children	$5.00	$3.00

Corvallis Gazette-Times

INTRODUCTION

Although we have both been gone from Corvallis for some 20 years, we are forever connected and indebted to the place, people and time we lived there. It's natural that the mind yearns to return, fitting that we would collaborate to honor this past, to bring together those poets—not-forgotten friends, associates and colleagues, comrades in verse—who shared it. The resulting *Voices of the Valley: An Anthology of Corvallis Poets* is much more than a long overdue acknowledgment of our fellow poets, as impressive a group as any the Pacific Northwest has produced. It has been our long-held belief that Corvallis was the hub of the poetry scene in the Willamette Valley, a literary oasis that fed us a steady stream of events, publications and inspiration. We hope that this anthology will help to enhance Western Oregon's literary tradition, while adding to the impressive list of anthologies and poets whose work defined the larger Pacific Northwest region. Perhaps other Oregon communities with a valued literary history will now be inspired to publish their own anthologies of local poets.

Voices of the Valley includes 32 poets who lived and/or worked in the Corvallis area—some for decades, a few their entire adult lives—who published widely and to acclaim, and who significantly impacted the local, the regional and even the national literary community as poets, teachers, editors and poetry ambassadors. We have focused here on the turn of the 21st century: the latter years (i.e., roughly the last decade) of the millennium through the first years of the current century since we consider that period a 'golden age' of local poetry. It was a time when readings, lectures, slams and themed literary events filled the calendar; when poetry groups and workshops, poetry outreach and poets-in-the-schools programs, publications and venues flourished; when listening to poetry was like hearing the heartbeat of the Willamette Valley. Because of our decade-long involvement with the Willamette Literary Guild, we were often at the center of it all, accomplishing a lot on a shoestring.

We have selected five poems from each contributor, or in several cases, the estates of poets who are no longer with us. Few of the poets are Oregon-born; most were transplants who were adopted as "one of our own" after settling in and making Corvallis their home. Most of the poems have some connection to Western Oregon or to the Pacific Northwest, its land, its people, its culture and events, and most were written during the time period we have identified.

The poets featured in the anthology include Chris Anderson, Sara Backer, Barbara Baldwin, Rachel Barton, David Biespiel, Dorothy Black Crow,

Richard Dankleff, Greg Darling, Be Davison Herrera, Eric Wayne Dickey, George Estreich, Linda Gelbrich, Charles Goodrich, Donna Henderson, Karen Holmberg, Steve Jones, Michael Malan, Jennifer Richter, Lex Runciman, Peter Sears, Matthew Shenoda, Steven Sher, Susan Spady, Michael Spring, Ann Staley, Clem Starck, Doug Stone, Anita Sullivan, Peggy Taylor, Linda Varsell Smith, Roger Weaver and Dale Willey. The group features honored teachers, editors and prize-winning poets, including Oregon Book Award winners and an Oregon Poet Laureate.

There are many more poets whom we could have selected, whose literary contributions helped define the community too, but the 32 herein were the most active—well beyond Benton County. Some of the notable poets (several were better known for their fiction/prose) not appearing in the anthology include Chris Gray, Ken Day, Haakon Hofstad, Jon Munster, Candace Paulson, Hollie Messenger, Beth Camp, Robert Crum, Jana Zvibleman, Elizabeth Campbell, Gregg Kleiner, Rick Borsten, (Abd) A.Y. Lafi, August Baunach, AliceAnn Eberman, Jessica Lamb, Wyn Schoch, Matt Yurdana and John Ginn. A larger retrospective of the Corvallis poetry scene would be incomplete without them and other talented writers and teachers.

The range of outstanding venues, organizations and publications that formed a home for Corvallis's formidable poets matched the variety of voices, complementing them well, while showcasing their poems before an enthusiastic public. You could find a packed event almost any night of the week at Grass Roots Books & Music, The Beanery, Old World Deli, The Corvallis Book Bin, The Corvallis Public Library, The Corvallis Arts Center, Oregon State University, Linn-Benton Community College, Benton Center, The Majestic Theatre, The Interzone or Uncle Hungry's.

Active literary groups and publications flourished in those years as well. These included the Willamette Literary Guild (events, series), CALYX Press and *Journal*, Cloudbank Books (and journal), *Fireweed* (Western Oregon journal), *ArtSpirit* (Corvallis Arts Center newsletter, featuring poetry calendar/pages), Oregon State University (*Prism*, visiting authors), Oregon State University Press, Linn-Benton Community College (*The Eloquent Umbrella*, The Valley Writers Series), Oregon Poetry Association (Willamette Valley branch), The Midway Theatre marquee, Mary's River poetry, Friends of William Stafford, The Majestic Theatre (Poets for Peace), Benton Center, *Pacifica: Poetry International* (*To Topos, To Topio*), *Riven Poetry Journal*, open unison stop, *Tcha teemanwi: Poems for Marys Peak, Marys River Poetry Anthology, River Songs, Let Us Drink to the River, The Mistry Guild*, Siski Press, Backer Editions, Benton County Writers, Willamette Writers, da Vinci Days, Marys Peak Poets, Arrowood Books, Airlie Press, *Willawaw Journal,* Hungry Society and ongoing poetry groups in people's homes led by Susan Spady, Dale Willey, Roger Weaver and others. These small weekly groups often stayed together for years. Some of the best poetry of the time was inspired and/or critiqued here. Some of the sessions became legendary.

Voices of the Valley includes a sampling of ephemera from that time period submitted by the poets, including press releases, promotional material, media clippings, publicity for featured events, journals and books, workshop and poetry group activities. These have been included to provide a context and to help those who didn't experience this local phenomenon to understand the extent of poetry's impact on the community.

The impact was significant. Some of the large-draw single events, prominently written up in the press (*The Corvallis Gazette-Times, The Albany Democrat-Herald, The Oregonian*), could attract hundreds of people. The regular reading series were popular, featuring local poets as well as 'name' poets from outside. These drew a steady audience too. Well-received events became celebrations of local life through poetry, the more memorable including 100 Years, 100 Writers: Celebrating Past and Present Corvallis-Benton County Writing, part of the Corvallis-Benton County Library centennial in 1999; Diverse Voices, celebrating the multicultural Corvallis poetry community in 1994; Poets of Faith, a post-9/11 gathering of poets in 2001; poetry slams at The Beanery; the annual Poets for Peace program at the Majestic Theatre; and the annual city-wide DaVinci Days, with its poetry activities each summer.

For all the public events that took place, Corvallis was at heart an incredibly close and nurturing literary community. Poets sought each others' critique, collaborated on writing and organizing events, developing projects and creating groundbreaking literary enterprises. Perhaps the most widely-known, bringing together poets and artists from around the country, CALYX started in 1976 as a collective feminist press founded by Corvallis writers.

This support was most evident whenever one of our own needed us. Just before the turn of the century, one of the poets included in *Voices of the Valley*, Peggy Taylor, whose health was steadily declining, was determined to see her book of poems published before she succumbed to cancer. It wouldn't have happened without help from the local poetry community, including a number of poets in this anthology who edited her manuscript and fast-tracked it at the printer's. And then, once the book was printed, it was quickly followed by a launch. Many people filled her back yard to hear her read her poems, buy her book, support her however we could. It was a beautiful sunny day. With her dream fulfilled, she went to lie down following the reading—people going in one by one to say a few words or spend a couple of minutes with Peggy. She was tired but clearly deeply moved by what seemed, according to one of the poets in attendance, like an ancient ceremony rather than merely a book launch.

Good poets evoke images of particular regions. Corvallis, the location, mattered, becoming a melting pot of voices, the one place on the map where we had all gathered to draw and share inspiration. Ultimately, these 32 strong voices shine enduring light on our corner of the Valley—even if many of us have since moved on. We are grateful that Roger Weaver, Ann Staley, Clem Starck, Dorothy Black Crow and Be Davison Herrera, who passed on during production of this book, will always be among us in the anthology. It took 20 years for this dream to take shape. We thank all the poets for making it real.

Special thanks to Linda Varsell Smith for being our eyes on the ground, for her invaluable suggestions, knowledge of and long history within the writing community. Thanks to Court Smith, Bob Frank, Anita Sullivan, Linda Gelbrich, Tom Booth at Oregon State University Press, Oregon State University Special Collections, Steve Jones, University of Oregon Knight Library Special Collections and CALYX Press, who were essential in locating poets, selecting and providing copies of poems and photos, securing permissions, providing material essential to the book. And thanks to the families and friends of Peter Sears, Susan Spady, Barbara Baldwin, Peggy Taylor, Richard Dankleff and Dale Willey. We have been encouraged by the universal enthusiasm for the project that we received.

Finally, this anthology is indebted to those who blazed the Oregon literary trail before us with groundbreaking anthologies that brought local writers to the public's attention and gave voice to regional identity. Anthologies from Verseweavers and Oregon Poetry Association come to mind. The Oregon Literature Series (1989–1995) with George Venn as general editor of the six (by genre) *From Here We Speak* volumes, was a national model (declared so by the NEA) that gave the region its literary bearings, Oregon's gatekeeper ushering lovers of literature through the turnstiles into the biggest arena. In 2016, another anthology edited by George Venn, *Beaver's Fire: A Regional Portfolio* (1970–2010), explored the range of Oregon's literary history, traditions and personalities, a compilation that leads to every writer who ever embraced the region.

We are hopeful that we can do the same for Corvallis-Benton County and the mid-Willamette Valley, that *Voices of the Valley* will set a standard for local poetry, while bringing joy to its readers.

Steven Sher
Michael Spring

July 2024

VOICES OF THE VALLEY

AN ANTHOLOGY OF CORVALLIS POETS

CHRIS ANDERSON

Photo courtesy of the poet

Chris came to Corvallis in 1986 to teach English at Oregon State University and has lived here ever since, retiring after 34 years at OSU. At first, he focused on the writing of essays. In 1993, he published a book of personal essays organized around his daily walks on the edge of the university research forest north of town where he lives, *Edge Effects: Notes from an Oregon Forest* (University of Iowa Press). But in the early nineties, he felt a call to ministry and started studying to become a Catholic deacon. Ordained in 1997, he has since served as a deacon at St. Mary's in Corvallis—simultaneously with teaching full time. In the mid-nineties, when he was studying theology at Mount Angel Seminary outside Salem, he started writing poems again after many years. Poetry is his first and abiding love. At the seminary, the poems just came pouring out again, in response to the joy and freedom that he was experiencing then. With the help of Peter Sears and Michael Malan, and with the financial backing of Tony Gorsline, he published his first book of poems in 2003, *My Problem with the Truth* (Cloudbank Books). Through Cloudbank Books, he helped create the Northwest Poetry Series, publishing books by Charles Goodrich, Lex Runciman and Paulann Peterson. A few years later, he joined Airlie Press, a mid-valley poetry collaborative, working with Donna Henderson, Jessica Lamb and a number of other poets to publish and promote two books of poetry a year, including his second book of poems in 2011, *The Next Thing Always Belongs*. As a member of Airlie Press, he began arranging and participating in readings and poetry events up and down the valley and in Portland, a number of them in Corvallis. In 2016, Stephen F. Austin State University Press published his third book of poems, *You Never Know*. Now he continues to walk in the forest as well as his daily practice of writing poetry. His being both deacon and poet are necessarily related. For him, "poetry is a form of spiritual testimony," as Stanley Kunitz puts it. "It comes in the form of a blessing."

Acknowledgments. The Soft Allegorical Woods (*America Magazine*); Paper Maple (*Ruminate*); The Neskowin Cottage Walk (*The Apple Valley Review; You Never Know*); Our Trip to Spokane for a Wedding (*Poetry Northwest; You Never Know*); We Who Move (*Switched on Gutenberg*).

The Soft Allegorical Woods

Roads lie buried here
in the forest that came before,
and sometimes you can find them,
up the long alder lanes
or down the lush wades of the giant ferns.

But if you get lost
just follow the gaps and traces
through the thickets and tangled
branches where deer step lightly
and bobcat pad or even—
if you look closely enough—
the tiny seams where
woodrat and vole have skittered
through the low, intricate topography
of this variable ground
you must solve like a crossword.

When the mud thickens
and the skunk cabbage leers,
you may even climb,
ducking and pulling through
cane brakes and vines,
up the steep sides of the hill
where a snag will give way
and you find yourself
falling, backwards, through air,
into the soft forgiving loam.
These things cannot hurt you.
These woods were made by falling.

No way is the wrong way.
You have been here before
and you are still here.
You can't go wrong
and you can't come out,
here in the soft allegorical woods.

Paper Maple

We bought the tree with the money I made when I baptized Stan,
who had nineteen confirmed kills in Viet Nam. He's an old man now,
in a wheelchair, shriveled and pale, and he wanted to be cleansed
of his sins. "I've been in hell," he told me, "and I want to be free,"

and though he didn't talk much, and could hardly move, when
I started to pour the water on his head, and I began to say the words,
"I baptize you in name of the Father"—"and of the Son," he said,
"and of the Holy Spirit," and the water dribbled down his face
and dripped off his chin, wetting the front of his pale, checked shirt.

We planted the tree on a fine spring day. The earth was soft
and warm. We dug the hole, scored the matted roots, and gently
set it in, then filled the hole with amended soil and watered,
thoroughly, soaking the ground until the bed had turned to mud.
It's a pretty tree. A Paper Bark Maple, they call it, because
the bark peels off in curly strips almost smooth enough to write on.

The Neskowin Cottage Walk

Montaigne was fifty-nine when he died. Not even
sixty. But I'm feeling fine, walking through one beach house
after another at the annual Neskowin Cottage Walk.
I love looking at other peoples' houses. The soft couches
and the shelves with their books and all the touching signs
of habitation. A coffee pot. A toaster. A vase of flowers
on a window sill. Why should we fear dying? Once
Montaigne was thrown from his horse. He raved and tore
at his doublet. But inside he felt a pleasure in gently letting go …
an infinite sweetness in repose. The smell of salt air.
The sound of waves crashing beyond the dunes, coming in
and going out. The fact is, he says, I was not there at all.

Our Trip to Spokane for a Wedding

I drive around town but don't remember where anything is.
My father is shrinking, he's getting smaller and smaller,
and he's losing his mind, too, I think. He says he gets in his car

and starts to drive but then can't remember where he's going,
and I'm no different. I keep making wrong turns, I keep getting lost,
and everything is changing anyway. Holy Cross
is now a daycare. The North Hill Public Library is a hair salon.

Driving back through the gorge I stop and climb to a waterfall.
There are hundreds of people on the paved path, and I resent them
at first, how fat they are and slow. But as we keep climbing

I start to join in the flow. All of our heads are bobbing, our arms
are swinging, and I think, the tall black man with the stiff knees
is my brother, the pretty little girl is me, and where else should we
be going but deeper and deeper into the shadows and the leaves?

At the top of the cliff we reach the waterfall, and the stream
is pouring over the edge, leaping and shining and scattering.
It's the Bridegroom! It's the Bridegroom, laughing!

We Who Move

I fall asleep in a room high above the sea.
That night a storm blows in, with heavy rains,
lashing the house again and again.
Once the wind slams so hard the bed jumps.

This really happens: the frame shudders, then stills.

Sitting in my office talking with a student
I suddenly feel dizzy. It's as if the building is swaying.
But then I realize, the building is swaying,
it's rocking, and the light hanging from the ceiling
is swinging back and forth, and it's as if
a wave of energy is rippling through the floor—no, is.

Sometimes it's not we who move.
Sometimes the angel really is an angel, not an allegory,
not a discourse, but with huge, dark wings,
heavy as suitcases, and my advice when an angel speaks
is to be very quiet. Hold very still.

If you sit long enough by a window,
early on a winter morning, you can see the moon
set into the dark trees, you can see it sink, very slowly,
every minute or so a little further, until finally
it disappears entirely, glowing in the tops of the fir.

Notice how the feathers overlap like herringbone.
Notice that Mary isn't holding a book.

SARA BACKER

Photo courtesy of the poet

Sara grew up in Worcester, MA, and Bend, OR, where she was stunned by the brightness of desert stars and the largeness of the mountains and sky. After completing a bachelor's degree in music at Oregon State University, she moved to California, first San Luis Obispo then, realizing her life was stuck at the age of thirty, to Davis where she completed a Master's degree in English, taking a poetry course from Gary Snyder. Looking back, she sees how tenacious his influence was on her poems—concrete imagery, a sense of place, a Chinese aesthetic of balance. A friend in Snyder's class, Eric Paul Shaffer, edited her first chapbook *Zillion to Zero Odds* (Longhand Press) in 1989. In 1990, Snyder connected her to a three-year position as Visiting Professor at Shizuoka University in Japan, where she had a view of Mt. Fuji from her second-floor apartment. She's still haunted by those frustrating, charming, lonely and magical years, and continues to write about Japan. When she moved back to Corvallis, she wrote her first (and only) novel, *American Fuji* (Penguin Putnam, 2001); the paperback was reprinted in 2009. She led mystery writing classes at Linn-Benton Community College and workshops in the Fooling Around with Words series run by Linda Smith, and joined a group of local poets that met in a coffee shop. While in Corvallis, she had poems published in *Poetry Northwest, Seattle Review, Poetry, Talus and Scree, RIVEN* and *Fireweed*. Sara returned to her native New England, where she still works as an adjunct instructor for UMass Lowell. Her second chapbook, *Bicycle Lotus*, won the 2015 Turtle Island Poetry Prize. She began to write speculative poetry, which was published in *Asimov's Science Fiction Magazine, Silver Blade, Apex & Abyss, Strange Horizons*, among others. Dancing Girl Press published her third chapbook, *Scavenger Hunt*, in 2018. In 2019, she received an MFA in poetry from Vermont College of Fine Arts and her first full-length book of poetry, *Such Luck* (Flowstone Press), appeared. Recent journal publications include *Crannóg* (Ireland), *The Rialto* and *New Welsh Review* (UK), *Not Very Quiet* (Australia) and American journals such as *The Pedestal Magazine, Turtle Island Quarterly, Journal of Compressed Creative Arts, Slant, Tar River Review, Cut Bank* and *Kenyon Review*. Sara took third prize in the 2019 Plough Prize for Poetry, received fellowships for writing residencies at Norton Island and Djerassi, and has been nominated for three Best of the Net and nine Pushcart prizes. In May 2019, she published an article about the Polish poet Ryszard Krinicki in the *The Writer's Chronicle*. She currently reads for *The Maine Review*.

Acknowledgments. Such Luck (*The Pedestal Magazine*); Jack (*Poetry*); The Drowning Man (*Poetry Northwest*); Your Egret (*Faultline*); Leaving the City Behind (*Turtle Island Quarterly*).

Such Luck

My California single girl bedroom:
cinderblock shelves, futon, paper globe light,
wine bottle candlesticks coated with waxy stalactites.
Lacking men to stay the night, I drank in bed. The more
I drank, the larger my glass grew. I waded surf with cabernet
in hand and yearned for love. Until I sipped and found a fish.

Fish! How did you get in my cup?
> *Jumped! Four feet straight up from snapping beaks.*
> *I could win the Fish Olympics!*

What should I do with you, Fish?
> *Don't dump me out! Those shags are hungry!*

Fish, how do you speak—and why?
> *Because you're listening! This is amazing!*

Are you real or imaginary?
> *Yes!*

Do you have some lesson to teach me?
> *No!*

What kind of fish are you?
> *A talking fish! The best kind!*

We talked till Fish's gills began to dry.
I walked the length of the longest pier,
far from gulls and cormorants, tossed
and watched him flip four times
before he dove into dark waves.
I tossed my goblet after him,
thinking how lucky I was
to be unlucky in love.

Jack

I have become the smaller flag on a ship,
the shorter rafters of a roof, a knave
in a pack of cards. I wear a skimpy coat,
tall leather boot, and leather drinking flask.
I am captured in a child's game
and hit when grown men gamble.
I am what they call a tame ape.

I was a common man
whose job was to lift weight.
Mechanical devices that replaced
my muscles took my job and pay
and more—they took my human name.
And I, who used to pull
my master's boots, hoist meat
and turn the spit, work the roller
and the winch, climb the steeple,
strike the bell and connect lines
in telephone exchange, am a daw,
the tiniest of crows, gathering
loose sticks to nest in castle ruins.

The solace of six centuries—and still—
is once, on a high and windy hill,
beside a well that was clear and full,
I kissed a girl named Gylle.

The Drowning Man

When he jumped over the railing of the bridge,
I jumped after him. That fast, that simple. I had
to find him in stagnant darkness, break him loose,
haul him to the noisy surface (not easy with water-
weighted coats and shoes), sidestroke him to land,
pinch his nose, tip his chin and force my breath twice
into his numb lungs. Two fingers below his sternum,
jab my palm on his diaphragm fifteen times.

The rescue squad chewed my ass, of course, always
call 911 first, never go in alone, I could have died myself.
Sensible advice for saving strangers, not husbands.
But tubed on the stretcher, foil blanket tucked around him,
going into the ambulance like a baked potato in the oven,
he looked like the stranger he had been all along.

Your Egret

The white bird stands
at your door. "I'm your egret."
You hold beer in one hand,
book in the other. You didn't
order an egret.

The egret shifts feet.
Snowball on wires.
Purity from a distance.
Up close, dirty feathers and lice.

You shut the door
and read and drink
all afternoon.

In your backyard, the egret
eats frogs:
plunge, snatch
—legs dangle from beak—
slurp, bulge.

You watch, afraid it will
clap wings
and chase you away.

The egret walks slowly.
"Don't go!" you call out. "You're
my egret!"
The white bird stops.
Vanishes.

Leaving the City Behind

The first city you picture when someone says *city*
is your love city, the one you learned by foot,
whose concrete abraded the soles of your shoes,

whose subway map still appears in your PET scan,
whose towers of glass skies and doorways of urine
revealed how rich rich people really are, how poor the poor.

You rented a studio: tiny floor, tall walls, curved window,
five locks on the door. You answered
phones, made copies, added numbers, poured coffee.

This city trained you to sense buses coming,
distinguish Bhutanese and Tagalog, to know
the taste of rabbit from goat.

In the daily treasure hunt of your love city,
you found an all-poetry bookstore with wing chairs
from a thrift store next to a neon stripper bar.

Gradually, you discovered you fell in love
with all your lovers because they were part of the city.
They flattened and shrank in the nearest field.

Leaving the city is not the same
as leaving the city behind.
You leave the city by car or ferry or phone.

You leave behind what has challenged and changed you
into someone able, at last, to follow a black swan
without fear—to become who you are outside of the city.

CALYX

A JOURNAL OF ART AND LITERATURE BY WOMEN

BARBARA BALDWIN

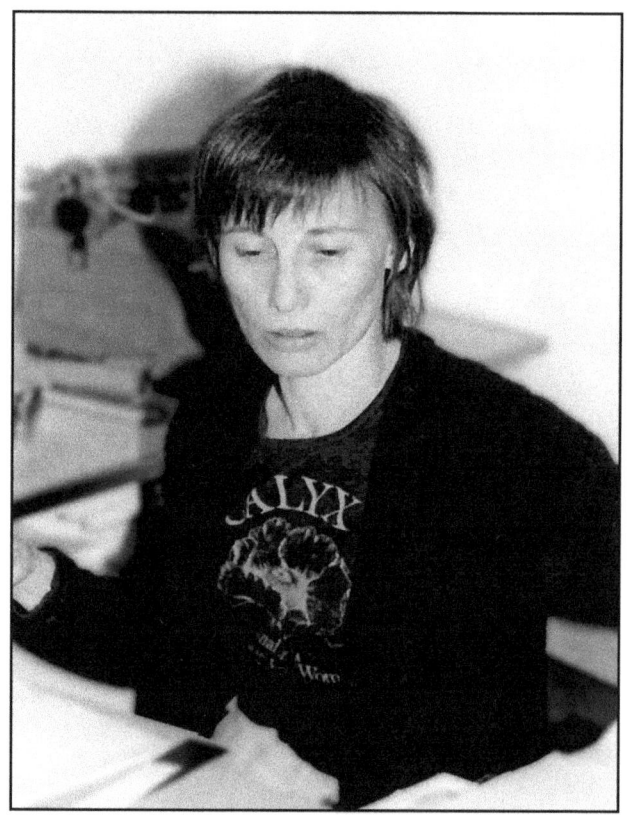

Photo courtesy of CALYX Books by permission of Rachel Baldwin

One of four co-founders of CALYX, Barbara died in 2017. Her posthumous collection, *Harvest*, was released in 2018 from CALYX Books. *CALYX Journal* was established in 1976 to provide a publication celebrating the excellence and diversity of women's literature and art. The books followed in 1986. At the start, production was done out of Barbara's Corvallis home. In the mid-1970s, Richard Dankleff invited her to join a local group of writers who met weekly to share their poems. The Friday night poetry group became a fixture of her life. She claimed that it was the crucible that led her to produce poems she could publish. Poetry had always been her emotional life. Now she came to admire the act and art of publishing itself. Barbara studied poetry with Carolyn Kizer, Madeline DeFrees and Scott Walker, who were enthusiastic about CALYX and offered practical input. Many women contributed their work to CALYX and told their friends about it: writers such as Diane diPrima and Olga Broumas as well as Carolyn Kizer. These poets recommended the journal to their fellow poets and students until the submissions to CALYX were not only prolific but reflected the finest work of the time. The editors established the editorial collective as the way to choose what to publish. They worked with a local printer. Barbara worked there as office manager and had hands-on experience producing the magazine from copy to finished publication. CALYX still occupies a studio in downtown Corvallis. As CALYX grew in both reputation and distribution, it began attracting volunteers to help staff the production. Barbara's poems appeared in publications such as *Fireweed*, *The Helicon Nine Reader* and *Negative Capability*. For 15 years, she edited and published rural economics and sociology for Western Rural Development Center's "Western Wire" at Oregon State University.

Acknowledgments. Aubade; For My Sister; Bessie (*Luckiamute*); Huérfano; August 1948. (All these poems appear in *Harvest*, CALYX Books; selected by Rachel Baldwin and CALYX Books.)

Aubade

Wake to rain. Wake to silence in the house
and a day plain as a pane of washed glass.
Light drifts across ceilings, now
in visible motion, now not, a supplemental
grey against grey walls. In this thin
nourishment, lean grass awaits
the wind's direction as my hinged bones
await what hauled them upright against
each cresting day.
                         They are gone. Anchor,
sail, and cargo, gone. Still I turn,
and the spruce turns on its great tap root
and the tulips turn. Through the window's wet
bulge, through eyes fat with loss, the white
day turns and wakes to the rain it slept by.

For My Sister

My sister is dead and I walk,
feet carrying legs carrying body
carrying brain, I walk in rhythm
with the beating of my heart
across a baked dirt path beside
stubble of cut wheat drying
in the heat of a white sun. I walk
through trees in the dark places
under branches, over damp earth
and moss I walk beside water,
yellow leaves floating on foam
reflecting yellow leaves. Moving
from shade to sun, I walk through
tall grass breaking in dry winds,
toward the western sun, I walk
in rhythm with the turning
of the earth.

Looking at the mountain
beyond patterns of fields and trees
reflecting yellow light and
brown and green, I stop and stand
in the light soaking into my skin
and my body opens, every pore
an eye, an ear, a mouth absorbing
the fields and trees and mountain.
Standing still looking at the
mountain standing still in
fields standing still in
light standing still on the
earth as it turns
I contain the moving universe
in my body standing still and
my sister is dead.

Bessie

In August the wheat field behind
our barn was burned and the land
lay unexpectedly flat
like a woman's belly after childbirth.

Grandmother was thirty-one
when her baby died of smallpox.
Before the child was buried
behind the barn with the others,
her husband left. He never looked back
at the garden of infant graves,
four children, a dry West Texas farm,
and his woman standing in the sun.

She wrung her hands,
the chickens' necks,
and burned the barn
because the sun said so.

Her spinster sisters
assigned her rage
to a madhouse,
four children to an orphanage,
and sold the farm,
erased the sun.

I was fifteen, believed my grandmother dead
when from her grave in Texas she said
"Please write." My father was an orphan
and could not answer. No one did. She died.

In August when the wheat field
flamed back at the sun,
black land ran flat like the rind
of a life, and smoke wreathed a requiem
for my grandmother, for mad women,
bad women, grieved, bereaved,
and left for dead women.

Huérfano

Carcass of a doe,
abandoned by some carnivore
in an open field.

Her body makes space for light
with slatternly ease.
Her clenched ribs grin.

Spiders
are spinning a wedding veil.
Webs float from her skull

like wings. The sun
bites her lip and surrenders.
Ghostly children dance.

Old women,
grey and trembling, walk
among trees and weep.

This is no marriage bed.
This emptiness we mend and mend
is wind that blows

between the legs of the stars.
These tenement bones
are accustomed to transience,

God
like a fat white cloud
waddling in and out.

August 1948

Chins and elbows spouted
into the sink like gargoyles,
mother, daughter, and grandmother
drip peaches hauled home still radiating
the summer day, their youth and love,
their all unknowing thrust into
this good taste, this warm fruit,
this circle of light in the swept kitchen
as if each lightly salted
mouthful were not the last.

RACHEL BARTON

Photo courtesy of the poet

Rachel's poetry is driven by voice, imagery and place, often couched in the natural world. After publishing several chapbooks—both of her students and of her own work (*Thunder Eggs and Other Poems; Alexander Yusha and Other Ghosts; Through a Black Moon; A Winter of Listening; So One Night; Among the Brambles; The Possibility of Sea*)—she launched *Willawaw Journal,* an online magazine of poetry and art. Peter Sears, who invited her to attend several of his poetry seminars and served as her mentor, was the keynote reader at the launch. With the launch in 2017, she released her chapbook, *Out of the Woods*. Another chapbook, *Happiness Comes*, was published by Dancing Girl Press in 2018. Two new collections, *This is the Lightness* (The Poetry Box, 2022) and *Jacob's Ladder* (Main Street Rag, 2024), are available through rachelbartonwriter.com. Besides serving as editor for *Willawaw Journal*, Rachel is an ongoing member of the editorial poetry collective for *CALYX Journal*, and reads for *Cloudbank Magazine*. She participates in a couple of critique groups and regularly attends the NW Poets Concord, the Oregon Poetry Association Conference and the Willamette Writers Conference. She has offered poetry workshops at Linn-Benton Community College (Corvallis) and also independently. The classes are generative as well as critical, modeled after the Writing Project in which the writer's voice is developed in a supportive community, culminating in the publication of individual chapbooks and public readings. Rachel also served as co-chair for the local chapter of Willamette Writers for two years, facilitating poetry workshops with this group as well as for OPA and NW Poets Concord, followed by a year as Assistant Editor in Chief for their *Timberline Review*. Rachel earned her BA in English at West Virginia University (1976), where she pursued graduate studies in art with a focus on printmaking. In 1978, she moved to Anchorage to continue her study of printmaking at the Visual Arts Center of Alaska. Moving to Oregon, she earned her Master's in Teaching from Western Oregon University in 2006. She taught English and ESOL, and facilitated the CRISS Literacy Project at Sweet Home High School. After enrolling in the Oregon Writing Project Summer Institute at Willamette University, she became a Teacher Consultant, and then completed the OWP's Advanced Poetry. Rachel's poetry publications include *Hubbub, The Oregon English Journal, Moon City Review, Main Street Rag, Sin Fronteras, Mom Egg Review* and anthologies such as *The Absence of Something Specified* and the OPA Pandemic Anthology. Her short stories can be found in *Blue Cubicle Press, Kindred Journal, BeZine* and *Clackamas Literary Review*.

Acknowledgments. If the Orange Cones Were Pawns I Would Be Queen (*Happiness Comes*); A Far Cry (*Mom Egg Review, Through a Dark Moon*); Slow Crossing (*Alexander Yusha and Other Ghosts*); Cameras in His Closet (*Alexander Yusha and Other Ghosts*); Stepping into the Wild.

If the Orange Cones Were Pawns I Would Be Queen

orange cones coax traffic to the far lane
a cluster of men with pressure hoses
transforms in broad swaths
the bridge's walk and railing
flogging the grit and grey of winter
from every surface and crevice

my own seasonal shift proceeds slowly
I must move beyond my comfortable sphere
of chicken dinners and sitcoms
step out where strangers meet and ideas collide
venture a story or line
beyond my living room

chess at the breakfast table
is a quick jump to defense
a greater mind than mine
fashioned this game
my son a better player
pushes me to see six moves ahead

I choose random
we're traveling to the train station
so it must be raining
the mist excites a halo of hair
I veer left but my passion
flies upward

A Far Cry

Teen takes his jacket and camera and his designer beverage. He is going up on the roof. No, he will not come down. It's not the top of the world but you can see it from there. If you drank a lot of Turkish coffee, you might see a thief enter Al Jebal's Bazaar wearing a balaclava. This is a college town, after all, where you can try anything once. He might steal the plastic crate on the counter full of baklava or the goat in the freezer. No, Chagall did not put him there. Nothing is flying in the air like lovers and a violin, not even a rooster, but something is in the air. I dream of the kid's closet. It is only a niche in the wall with shelves narrower than a sock. His grey clothes are stuffed onto the ledges haphazardly. He is not yet established.

He climbs to the roof, dull thuds to my pen's scratches, then silence. I suppose we all want to climb or fly to a high place sometimes, up the mountain to an untouched dome of sky. From there I can see the glacier's run-off—a braided river frozen in swirls and humps as if only yesterday or a moment ago it ploughed pell-mell across the valley. I carry my high place within but he is still young and searching. Cows calve and so do icebergs but in the valley of now we're talking orchards or the Old Growth Trail up Vineyard Mountain. This is a far cry from Turnagain Arm, where Dall sheep and their kids climb the cliffs on narrow rock ledges, and sheep gazers crane their necks to spot the curved tusks, the scampering white coats.

Slow Crossing

morning fog never lifts for him
fog out the back door is as reluctant
hiding the garden's woody vines
the sentries of cedar and maple
the idea of a river the quiet of high water

some complaining motor of a boat
whines closer then recedes
no lanterns at the forest's edge
to illuminate the snag the sink hole
just a muffled fog of worries

we keep the lights on all day
the grey light at the window never changes
I'm guessing the wine-colored shadow
beneath the naked plum
leaves and a scattering of twigs

in his fog the sacred icons in a secret room
photos of his sister his mother's sewing machine
he dreams at the edge of the Willamette
blanketed in a fog like the ethers
between here and the hereafter

Cameras in His Closet

he used to polish his precious camera lenses
until the black felt cloth grew thin and shredded
infiltrated the interstitial spaces
became black birds on a far horizon
his eyes too weak to see them

steam punk knobs on the Rolleiflexes outfox
him in his fog of dementia he damages them
beyond repair as he cranks an empty case or
winds film from another dimension another century clicks
the shutter at the window's view hoping
to catch an eagle in the snag across the water

for years he kept to himself stayed out of doors
platting the spread of tussock moth and spruce beetle
he wandered the Siuslaw Three Rivers Three Sisters
his feet carrying him down riverbanks and up
ridges to high country

his kitchen his dark room when he was able-bodied
his photos fill Forest Service drawers
pepper the archives of National Geographic
a thick stack stuffs the box under his desk
he remembers them like yesterday no
like Tokyo's Mt. Fuji like his mother's cabbage soup

Stepping into the Wild

we have confined the glorybower
to the far side of the drive
rigid cement at least slows the errant runners
a skittish kind of taming (the blueberries at risk)

cucumbers clamber over the sides of their bed
fill the space between with lush leaf and vine
the benign fruit grows fat or lop-sided
pale yellow or deep green as it pleases

tomatoes chocolate heirloom and cherry
grown taller than me thrive in their modest crib
densely leaved and fruited the yellow toms
win the prize for highest yield

at season's end they spill over the borders
onto the mulch into the lawn
and when I go to pick a bowl full
sliding my arm into that fragrant tomato jungle—

I reach into the wild part of myself—
hair disheveled cloaked in green
yellow toms adorn my earlobes like gems
button close my green jerkin

DAVID BIESPIEL

Photo courtesy of the poet

David is the author and editor of over a dozen books of poetry and prose, including *Beautiful Is the World: New and Selected Poems: 1996–2026*. Since 2001, he has been poet-in-residence at Oregon State University where he teaches in the graduate Creative Writing Program. Poet, critic and memoirist, David is the founder and president of Portland's Attic Institute of Arts and Letters. His memoirs include *A Place of Exodus: Home, Memory, and Texas* (Kelson Books, 2020) and *The Education of a Young Poet* (Counterpoint Press), selected as one of Poets & Writers Best Books for Writers in 2017. His poetry books are *Republic Café* (University of Washington Press, 2019), *Charming Gardeners* (UW Press, 2013), *The Book of Men and Women* (UW Press, 2009; Oregon Book Award; Poetry Foundation's Best Books of the Year); *Wild Civility* (UW Press, 2003); *Pilgrims & Beggars* (Portlandia Books, 2002); and *Shattering Air* (BOA Editions, 1996; Oregon Book Award finalist). *A Long High Whistle: Selected Columns on Poetry* (Antilever Press, 2015) received the Frances Fuller Victor Award for General Nonfiction. He was editor of *Long Journey: Contemporary Northwest Poets* (Oregon State University Press, 2006), which received a Pacific Northwest Booksellers Association Award. Additionally, David's poetry and prose have appeared in *The New Yorker, The New Republic, American Poetry Review, New Republic, Partisan, Slate, Poetry* and *The New York Times*, among other publications. He is a contributing writer for *Politico* and poetry columnist for *The Republic*; since 2002, he has written the Poetry Wire column for *The Rumpus*. From 1995 to 2000, he was the editor of *Poetry Northwest*. David has been the recipient of National Endowment for the Arts, Lannan and Stegner fellowships; and has twice been a finalist for the National Book Critics Circle Award's Nona Balakian Citation for Excellence in Reviewing. Raised in Houston, TX, he earned his MFA at the University of Maryland, where he studied under Stanley Plumley and Michael Collier.

Acknowledgments. Room (*Poetry; Republic Café*); The Theory of Hats (*Poetry; The Book of Men and Women*); A Man Feels the World; Though Your Sins Be Scarlet (*Slate; The Book of Men and Women*); With Passing Wonder I Notice the Tracks of an Animal (*Academy of American Poets' Poem-a-day*).

Room

After it came in like a dark bird
Out of the snow, barely whistling
The notes *father, mother, child,*
It was hard to say what made us happiest.

Seeing the branches where it had learned
To stir the air? The air that opened
Without fear? Just the branches
And us in a room of wild things?

Like a shapeless flame, it flew
A dozen times around the room.
And, in a wink, a dozen more.
Into the wall, the window, the door.

You said the world turns to parts.
You said the parts are cunning spheres.
You said you always love the face of sin.
You said it's here, the lips and eyes and skin.

Outside the snow deepened
With heaves of discontent.
Inside, the tremor of our life
Flew in and in and in.

The Theory of Hats

It is hard even to admit this theory of hats, that to wear
The faithless one brimmed tightly over the eyes—
The featherless and discreet one, a hat with a secret code
That says, *To spoil the child is to fatten the serpent*—
To wear that hat (imperfectly as a crow's crown) against the sun
Is to bear the ruins of the unborn into our hearts—
He, shouting at the brunt of trees;
She, shifting like a seer to restore them.
It is hard to know happiness with a hat like that.
Or to forget the pangs sung with such burly impatience,
Or to heal the blurred things and soft hurts.
Even the blind self becomes a dervish, what with the torsion
And the far-off *vita nuova* like a new virus or virtuoso,
What with the tussles and old, pure-lit suppressions.
Then to be surprised by joy: Like the last rain of summer,
The big, spiraling, wounded animal of rain
With no place to turn, drumming the brown grass,
Rain falling without meaning, but perfectly faithful,
Into the petals of wind and the unopened roots—
Such tenderness looked to, like love, but unquestioned.
Then some afternoon with the sky lifting off again,
She will come to sit on the porch like a dark sparrow
And let the sun creep slowly onto her hair
And grow old and wonder about the balance of things.
And he beside her, sitting, too, distracted in the sun for hours,
But all the same, both of them, at last, so much warmer.

A Man Feels the World

> for Tomas Tranströmer

The gray, green sky—infinite in
The leafed-out tips of the leaves—
And the sun, set upon the heights,
Flat as a birthmark, a singe, or
Wound from a stack of burnt
Wood brightening into smoke,
Like the wisps of the first
Weeks after a death, or two
Deaths—after the heart goes
To root and branch—or
Like longing for the details
Of light veins in leaves, in
Heavy-headed grasses of spring, or
Light-headed petals of a daisy, in
Order to shine a light on the last
Good wish you made. Show me:
Dust rising in shadow, or the bell
Curve of a bay, gravel of a bare
Stream, where, once, an ocean's
Beginnings blurred under the
Sweltering waves of insects. And
Yet, here, where it's easy to
Notice the tang in the wet
Air, the sky doesn't open,
Nor turn whiter, ascending,
Toe-hold by toe-hold, the
Way I used to climb a tree,
Wedging into the fat,
Parental, crook of
Branches, with a raw
Silence of deduction, and
At the soul-poured out,
Suffering end of affection,
When I'd long for
My own name, weathered

As a thumb, I'd lean, chin
Raised, far out under the
Gossamer pulse of the sky.

Though Your Sins Be Scarlet

It didn't start with the phenobarbital or the reefer,
The ironweed or the magnetic force of a gentle woman.
It started with a voice saying *return* that I could not hear,
And the nineteen *Amidahs* did nothing for transgressions.
Scarletted-up—all those years—I fiddled and giggled
And got muscle-bound as a deaf dreamer, a striper,
A pressed-against pirate, got teary and ripe with the scuttled
Worry coming back again and again, and no winners
To speak of, no vintage TV to settle in with like sins
Of the zodiacal light or kissing cousins or crummy laws.
I haven't been called a weak sister, and I don't mean to, that's plain.
But the rummy tumblers, the bloody knuckles, I'll crawl
For them. I'll crawl. And the cutting up and the swear words—
Such crimson no wool can wrap around. Look unto the lamp black
And see givers and campy gents and you'll forgive anything hard.
I have. Remember? It was just after she left, burning the last wick.

With Passing Wonder I Notice the Tracks of an Animal

It comes out of the language of nothing I recognize
Though it is something in you, at least as I keep
                              looking at you
And you turn back to me. I ought to have guessed
From the simple order of the tracks that you knew
Without looking what place in the wild night
The animal came from,
            and through which of our windows
It has looked into, sometimes with an eye
On our waking, other times on our sleeping
                          with the doorways open
Where, I suppose, the spirits of the defeated
Appear, white as lakes, carrying maps to someplace
Ahead of us, running now, and now you running,
And the animals guiding your footsteps,
Like a flake of snow,
You, without a single acquaintance among the spirits,
Or understanding, you so solitary in your running.
                          And then the return—
And I assume you have nothing to say
And that if I wait there'll be only the waiting
Then nothing but a moment of darkness
And a surprising order stirring in the head
Shaking off the early morning cold.
Then all at once a door closing,
               an hour of answerless letting go
Like a last hammer of blue sky
Cracking the light.

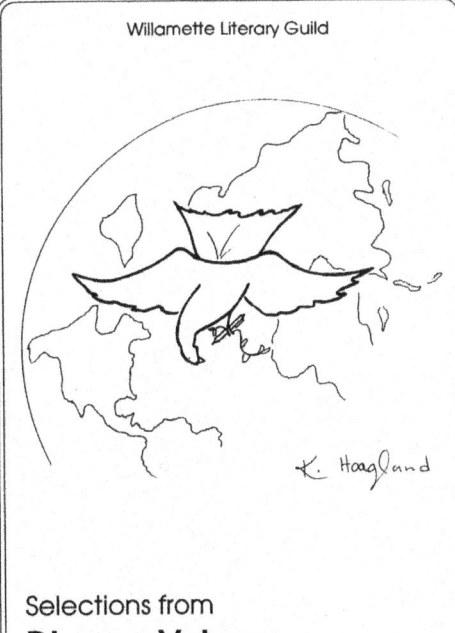

DOROTHY BLACK CROW

Photo courtesy of the poet

Dorothy attended Oberlin (BA, 1957), Yale (MA, 1958) and the University of Michigan (PhD, Linguistics, 1969). She taught high school English (Roslyn, NY), GED classes (Point Park College, Pittsburgh, PA), College English (Catholic Girls College, Kalamazoo, MI) and College English & Engineering (Illinois Institute of Technology, Chicago, IL). After she married Lakota spiritual leader Selo Black Crow, she moved to Wanblee, SD, where she raised a sacred bison herd. Dorothy taught in the College English & MAT Program at Oglala Lakota College (1977–1988), followed by College English & Native American Studies at Linn-Benton Community College (1988–2001). She also taught senior classes of "Write Your Life Story" in Corvallis, Philomath, Tangent, Albany and Mennonite Village (1988–2000); and College English & Native American Literature at Oregon Coast Community College (2001–2015). From 1988–2020, she was a member of Willamette Writers in Portland; a founder and board member of the Willamette Writers Coast Branch (2005–2015); a member of Writers on the Edge (1998–2018); chair for two years and subsequently yearly program chair of the Oregon Poetry Association (2013–2018); and *Tuesdays* poetry weekly in Waldport (1998–2020). A book of her poems, *Anuk-Ite' Double-Face Woman Poems*, was published in 2012. She has published more than 50 poems, fiction, creative nonfiction and memoir. She has also authored *The Handless Maiden: A Lakota Mystery.* Dorothy writes to honor the elders and record the passing of a culture, sharing its loss and encouraging its retrieval. She believes that the culture can be revived through storytelling, which binds and heals, changing the way people think of Native Americans, specifically American Indian Movement (AIM) leaders. For her, the Spirit World is real and powerfully present, whether we sense it or acknowledge it. Living on Pine Ridge Reservation, she experienced this many times. Dorothy is presently finishing her third mystery, *Peyote Firebird*.

Acknowledgments. Songs to the Sea; Wave after Wave, Sea-Breathing; Whatever Grows in Salt Air; Hold Fast; Believe in the Ocean. (All these poems are from a new unpublished poetry collection.)

Songs to the Sea

I never look for a lover. I am one.
James Broughton

1.
When I cannot sleep, I stare at your swell
caught in the moonlight out on the point.
Soft as silver shushing below me,
your shimmering spirit calls:
climb down to the tide pool shelf
and I will froth your feet, gently
as the sea fans waving in my surge.

Beside me anemone and starfish
cling to the lava, braced for the curl
and swish of the surf.
Broken mussel shells gleam,
and I am restless as the shuddering sea.

2.
The way one small curl
of green-eyed sea
glows from the afternoon sun, your
translucent face pulled silky thin,
I long to lick your polished jade,
riffle your long kelp strands,
caress your backside curl,
ride your foaming crest—then
slide down your trough and sink
beneath your pounding surf,
sea foaming.

3.
You called me and I said maybe.
You gave me jade and I said yes
you pulled me down
deep
brought me to the edge

of dissolution
churned me up amid sea palms
and barnacles
scoured raw and clean.

4.
To feed your hunger
I bring you bones of salmon
salmon berries black caps salal
bouquets of sea lavender
sea holly statice sea thrift
You suck my offerings under
and thrash for more.

5.
I will not go down today
your face severe and cold
how could I have ever loved you
even while you surround me.

I lean my back against sharp lava
black and solid as when it seethed
into your wide mouth eons ago.

I taunt you with songs
glower at your gray mist
shiver at your cold caress
spray rising from the rocks
I will not go down
to your salty dusk
yet your soul seeps
into mine.

6.
Now that I am old, the sea is my lover.
I have stroked beyond male and female,
swum beyond the breakers and kelp beds,
dived underneath lava rocks into caves.

I long for a love as wide as the sea
whose breath slows my surging heart.
You call to me, offer your mist and foam.
Were you a man, I would lie down for you.
Were you a woman, I would suck your breasts.
I grow vast and deep to embrace you,
my bed shudders from your force,
       if not this wave
       then the next.

Wave after Wave, Sea-Breathing

Surfers snort at him who says
"Seen one wave, seen 'em all!"

Not for me, nor my grandma
who painted wave after wave
to catch the curl, jade-thin
and luminous sheen and
sea foam frothing on the sand.

Her oil seascape catches
the roar of long trenchers
rolling in thousands of miles
endlessly even while
we sleep, sea-breathing.

Sea-reaching, yearning,
clutching the sand and wave-curl
calling to those who die and don't
drown but sink to the bottom
of the sea where the
Salmon People live.

If we stay we drown
pounded by surf against rock
until our salt-air becomes
salt in our blood.

Whatever Grows in Salt Air

They told me nothing would grow here,
too close to the sea
where sou'westers blast in the winter
and cold Arctic air in the summer, mists studded with salt,
oceanfront-once-removed
on the cliff north of Cape Foulweather
thin acid soil over black basalt.

But I saw all around me
invasive species
Scotch broom, knotweed. Joe Pye weed, wild onion
burdock and brambles
and native species
salal, ferns,
filled the lots by the sea.

So I studied horticulture: *hali*
the salt-tolerant plants and names
sea thrift, sea holly, sea lavender, sea aster
planted whatever I liked
watched it die and come back:
fennel, comfrey, borage, calla lilies and crocosmia
wild iris, yellow violets, *frittilaria*, bergenia, hebe, escallonia
wild onion, miner's lettuce, wild geraniums, lithodora
forget-me-nots, Japanese anemone, phlox
festoon the lots overgrown

ocean meadows untouched by lawnmowers
belonging to ODOT the People

so I knew something would grow if I let it go
rather than root it out for
dahlias and hostas—feast for slugs
corn, cukes and peppers—feast for rot
bulbs for voles

Whatever grows, let it stay, migrate across the driveway
expand and take over the garden
kale, chard and parsley reseed across the road
even lilies and clematis protected from the wind.

Whatever grows in salt air,
let it be.

Hold Fast

A colony of *Postelia*—sea palms—clings
to the rocks below Cape Foulweather

washed by a rogue wave   dark
green fronds dance in the wind
amid a rush of foam, suck of tide

Hold fast
to rocks once lava hissing into the sea
roots so strong no sea crest can loosen

Hold fast
tide in, tide out, day and night, year after
year *Postelia* fed by a rogue wave
surge of life—diatoms and wetness

without the tides *Postelia* and we
will perish

Hold fast:
We are grieving

two teenagers swept off the rocks at Smelt
Sands Beach by a rogue wave

honeymooners swept off the rocks at South
Jetty by a rogue wave

Believe in the Ocean

> *Even the upper end of the river*
> *Believes in the ocean.*
>   William Stafford

I believe in the ocean.
What's not to believe?
150 yards below my door,
horizon high as wainscoting
around an endless room of sky.

When you go down to the beach
the ocean's at eye-level, tame
even with tidal surge and spume,
but if you climb to the top of
Cape Foulweather, the sea rises
higher and higher with each step.

My sister-in-law Agatha Tall Mandan
came from the South Dakota plains
to see if the ocean her brother
sailed on for 29 years was real.

When I drove her over the last hill
on Route 20 down into Newport
she grabbed the car door handle,
hung on for fear of drowning.

Forget about sneaker waves,
neap tides and tsunamis. That huge
wall of water ahead, right here in
Newport, rose up to swallow her.

We'd call her *naïve, uneducated.*
But I say she believes in the ocean.

RICHARD DANKLEFF

Photo by permission of OSU Special Collections & Archives Research Center

Richard was born in Nebraska and attended the University of Nebraska before serving in World War II. He continued to serve in the US Merchant Marines until 1950, and in the US Army in 1951 and 1952. After the war, he completed a BS at Columbia University (1949). He earned an MA from the University of Nebraska (1954) and a PhD from the University of Chicago (1959). From 1963 until his retirement in 1987, he was a faculty member in the Oregon State University English Department. In addition to his teaching responsibilities, he wrote poetry and led a poetry workshop in the Corvallis community. He continued to mentor other writers of poetry after his retirement. Richard's poetry was published in journals such as *American Scholar, Carolina Quarterly, College English, Hiram Poetry Review, Kansas Quarterly, New Republic, Poetry Northwest, Prairie Schooner* and *Sewanee Review*. He is the author of three poetry collections. *Popcorn Girl* (1979) and *Westerns* (1984) were published by the Oregon State University Press. *Off Watch* was published by Oregon Sunrise Press in 2001. Richard died in Corvallis in 2010.

Acknowledgments. Flute Song (*American Scholar*); Adah (*Prism*); Lt. Montgomery Pike Harrison (*Kansas Quarterly*); When the Stars Fell; Grasshopper Summer (*Arvon Foundation* – 1980 Anthology). (All these poems are included in *Westerns*, Oregon State University Press.)

Flute Song

'Twas a curious fact that when Judge Russell played
his flute at night, his horses came and stood
on the cabin porch. When the music soared they paid
such careful heed they seemed to gauge the mood
and quality of tone. Clear nights, wet nights they stayed
and stamped a few times when an extra good
sustained diminuendo that would fade
and seem forever lost (the flute might brood,
as if the Judge were sorry or afraid)
came flowing back crescendo in a flood
of notes as bold as warblers trill when shade
or leaves conceal the singer. Soft or loud,
the Judge's hermit-thrush arpeggios could pervade
so tenderly the Cascade solitude
that daybirds, wakened, may have long delayed
to sleep again (they were so sweetly wooed)
and ghosts of ladies may have tried to wade
the deep horse-pasture creek but, baffled, cooed
forlorn cadenzas back across the glade.
Seldom did a nicker or stamp intrude
upon the solo flute. And the nags obeyed
a strict decorum. When nature called, they would
walk off a decent way and stand; they made
even those tall-high interludes
slow and stately, in deference to the serenade.

Adah

That sound like coyotes may be (when the wind
is this direction) old Adah calling her pigs.
She's a strong mistruster of folks. As for the pigs,
although they wallowed in the river mires
they had nothing to do with those olden
devil-ridden swine. In her sodbusting prime
Adah would have ordered off the place
any fool that called her pigs unclean. Some nights

it slips her mind the bank drove off all her stock.
What does get caught in her head is fear – that thieves
are after her boar and sows. She'll start for the river,
calling out the ancient names they honored
all those years, when she sold none of her beasts
except some litters. That cry sounds run-together
but a hunter walking over her way tonight
might make out that red boar's name *Ab-
salom* ... or *Ra-chel Le-ah Ra-chel.*

Lt. Montgomery Pike Harrison

Because he rode a beautiful sorrel
over the ridge alone,
his blue uniform shining and
his brown hair long on his neck,
some Kiowas shot the Lieutenant,
scalped and stripped him, carried off
even his boots and socks.

Because his dead grandfathers
were General Zeb Montgomery Pike and
the General Harrison who was,
for a month, President,
the lieutenant's judicious c.o.
had the bare corpse
thickly coated with tar and
packed between layers of charcoal
in a sealed wagon-box coffin
that the soldiers escorted—"without
inconvenience"—northeast
42 days over plains thick with
mesquite, through a Texas norther
that killed 33 of their mules, across
branches, forks and tributaries
of the Brazos, the Trinity and the Red
to Fort Smith, Arkansas
to be buried with military honors.

When the Stars Fell

That muddled next forenoon
the crabby medicine man
(still cross, pox scars dabbed
scarlet) rode off north fast
to talk with more skywatchers.
The dogs prowled stiff-legged.
Painted to fight, the men
rode their horses single file
round and round the camp.
Women wailed death chants.
As if gone mad, the dogs
began to howl like wolves.
Excited children (grandmother
could remember), forbid
to stray, made up a game
in which red stones
were falling stars
and red-mud-smeared children
were scabby medicine men
watching *ai-yee* the sky
with scowls.

Grasshopper Summer

She rushed between her pumpkin patch and cellar
brushing a mass of hoppers from each armload
of green pumpkins. In a voice he hardly knew, she called
to the boy to sweep the sides of the house. Slipping
on greasy hoppers, she pushed the cow to the shed
and walked on hoppers back to the house and sat.
The boy followed her in to ask if bugs
would burn, but got no answer. Home from the field,
his dad, cursing low, brought in clothes
left out on the line and made two trips for harness.
He vetoed fire, "Too many burn." She sat.
His dad waited; then said "Corn's gone"; then caught
some hoppers on top the table and pinched their heads.
Inside, they hardly heard the sound,
and did not have to watch, though the clouds were still
drifting in from the west. His dad said, "I'll light
the lamp." She stared at the floor.
"That hum," his dad asked, "is that their wings
or jaws?" She wouldn't speak; next day
the same; and on to fall … few words.

GREG DARLING

Photo courtesy of the poet

When not writing poems with a pen, Greg might be found casting for steelhead and salmon with a fishing rod or helping friends with gardening. Insofar as poetry, he enjoys experimenting with different forms and personas, and appreciates the intricate relationship between humanities, science and the environment. His interest in poetry began in high school and he continued to write as a philosophy major at Oregon State University and in the decades since. Even as a founding partner of Corvallis Cyclery, he found time to write. Born in Spokane, Washington, Darling has lived in Corvallis since 1970, the year he enrolled at OSU. Through the years, he hosted writers workshops where participants critiqued Richard Dankleff's poetry and contributed to *CALYX Journal*; assisted in the opening of the Corvallis Arts Center; and as a bicycle mechanic participated in the da Vinci Days festival. He has been a fixture at The Beanery coffee shop downtown, where he often wrote and sometimes read his poetry. At the beginning of the millennium, he was a member of the Hungry Society. At present, you may find him socializing at a local coffeehouse.

Acknowledgments. Fire and Ice; Immigrant; Truck; A Ponderance; Letter to Celeste from the Great North Woods. (All these poems are previously unpublished.)

Fire and Ice

For less than what we love, looks turn to stone;
whole winters slide like bridges under ice;
rooftops freeze and gutters split until
most welcome springtime triumphs once again …
so it is with the thawing season,
the burgeoning season; hot on the heels of ice …
fur collar or lilac bloom, my love?
Words dart like little birds through frozen fields;
The timeless melting meadow survives …
lost thoughts renew companion charm,
think neither here nor there, my dear …
love's best when kissed, held in arms,
from ice to fire now ever speed wended love,
from you … from you … this heat … this fire!

Immigrant

Crying to the crowd
hat in hand …
no one can refute
the wheel barrow,
the two-wheel cart,
the cassion …
anyone can refute the desperation
of a human being

Carry only
what is necessary
they tell me.
Refuse to play
the game of "hearts."
Touch base
with a quiet vengeance.

This is not the first time
you will hear this.
Something tells me
it's not the last.

Walk softly, my love …
Walk softly.

Truck

Hot sun, hot sky, grinding
up a dry summer switchback
to the hilltop wheatfields,
Umatilla County. White dust
choking to axle-height, not sure
we can make it up the grueling
grade for the fifteenth and final
day of harvest, Brake drums
grinding, grinding, tires
grabbing rock, slipping, grabbing
rock … only one broken axle
this year on the two-ton GMC.
Three months back and this road
was a solid winding track. Chewed
to loose, dry dust … so close
to finishing the harvest … twelve
hundred acres of dry land wheat
off the tops … 45 to 50 bushels
per acre, a sparse yield of
dry land wheat … it will be nice
to get back to the Willamette Valley
in time for the salmon run.

A Ponderance

I see shadows pressed
against the face of the moon
and moonlit trees and grasses
along the east pasture woodland
dressed in a deep blue
and purple garb
melting into
the darkness, the night, the stillness
of nothing's nothingness … I hear
the babbling creek.

A breeze pushes
against my shirt, my face. One
day these, too, will move towards
stillness, the depth of turning,
turning deep within … Will you
be ready for that? Will I?
Those steeped in chagrin, remorse,
self-punishment; they move as constant,
always forward, as I, walking along
the east pasture boundaries
in playful darkness.
Am I one to keep pace with that?

Letter to Celeste from the Great North Woods

Let's find a median in ourselves,
talk sense to one another.
Too many myths, too many sacred
chants, obfuscating hieroglyphs,
petroglyphs. The words of old and
the words of new blend into
such a hollow, self-precious
point of view. We assent
and we commit to the vagaries
of our undecided predicament.
Life? I'll call it that.
Meaning? Give me a minute …
I'll think of something.
So it is we look into the mirror
and say: "Yes! That's it! That's
exactly what I saw!"
One day, Celeste, you too
must come in from the cold.
Only the fire, the food, the
warmth in the study shall
keep us warm. Outside the
smallest things in life
do truly matter.

ERIC WAYNE DICKEY

Photo by Joseph Ohmann-Krause

Eric Wayne Dickey holds a MFA in Creative Writing (2009) and an Honor's BA in English and Philosophy (1998) from Oregon State University. He was a board member of the Willamette Literary Guild from 1999–2001, for which he organized the "Poets for Peace" reading event in Corvallis in response to the September 11th attacks, and several events honoring William Stafford. Together with Michael Spring, he co-edited *Riven Poetry Journal* in the early 2000s. As editor for *Pacifica: Poetry International (formerly To Topos: Poetry International)*, he received grants from Oregon Literary Arts in 2005, 2008 and 2018. Eric received an honorable mention in the 2021 Angela Consolo Mankiewicz Poetry Prize contest by Lummox Press for three poems from *The Book of James*. His poem "Upon Watching a Reenactment of a Civil War Battle" won the Academy of American Poets Roger Weaver Undergraduate Award in 1998. The poem was also used during a formal ceremony honoring the return of the reclaimed remains of a Civil War officer. He is a John Anson Kittredge Fund for Individual Artists grant recipient, administered by Harvard University, and a Vermont Studio Center Fellow. Eric has published two books of poetry, *The Hardy Boy Poems* (Beard of Bees, 2013) and *Forgive Me, Tiny Robots* (Argotist Online, 2013), and a children's book, *Alex the Ant Goes to the Beach* (Craigmore Creations, 2014). His new poetry collection, *The Book of James*, is forthcoming in July 2026 from Finishing Line Press. Erica Goss interviewed him about the book for her newsletter, *Sticks and Stones* (January 2021). He has poems and translations in *PageBoy, Contrary Magazine, Cloudbank, Lummox, Rhino, Blazevox, Talking Writing, Truck* and *On Barcelona*. He is a 2021 Pushcart Prize nominee for his poem "James Dean," which appeared in *Contrary Magazine*. Eric works as a grant proposal developer with the Division of Extension and Engagement at Oregon State University.

Acknowledgments. Upon Watching a Reenactment of a Civil War Battle (*To Topos: Poetry International*); Pretzel Legs (*Freeway: Poems*); After You Left (*Freeway: Poems*); James Dean (*contrarymagazine.com*); Face on the Floor (*talkingwriting.com*).

Upon Watching a Reenactment of a Civil War Battle

His pen moved across the page
as it did one hundred sixty years ago,
and he spoke of dead ideas,
preventing them from fully disappearing.
Would he himself die by his own free will?

Or, when the freedom fighters came,
did he hide in the darkened closet
with mirrors unreflecting the inside?
Or was he the one that lay riddled
with round bullets among the many bleeding men?

If so, did he open his eyes one last time
to see the peach blossoms of the orchard—
the battle ground—falling early
from the many flying bullets,
falling like snow over his body, his face, his eyes?

Pretzel Legs

My legs are a braided pretzel,
my dreams run loose in the streets.

A dog tries to take a bite of me
before its leash jerks it away.

I untie my legs,
stretch like a runner.

Strangers call for me to hurry.

Around us, the whole world
casts an uneasy eye

and starts like buffalo
through open prairie—

houses, cars, trees, honking horns,
diesel exhaust, clouds, wind:

everything, everything running!

After You Left

I stopped exercising and riding my bike.
Instead, I drove to work every day.
I stopped eating oatmeal, only eggs
over easy and buttered toast for breakfast,
hamburgers and French fries for lunch,
and a strict liquid diet for dinner.

I drank lots of coffee and beer,
smoked cigarettes and cigars,
went to bars and flirted with women.
And I admit, the scent of an unfamiliar
perfume behind an ear tickled my nose.

I didn't do laundry, make the bed,
or open the curtains. The dishes stacked up.
I didn't recycle, sweep the house, or even take out
the garbage. I forgot to feed the dog
on occasion. She now looks at me
with drooping ears and licks at my feet.
The cat hisses at me when I walk by
and hasn't been around much.

I hardly brushed my teeth or showered,
stopped flossing altogether,
and stayed up late watching TV
and eating chocolate ice cream.

I took your advice after you left
and really let myself go to hell.

James Dean

>for James David Dickey, March 3, 1966 – October 22, 2008

>*Men cry from the grave while they still live
>and now I am this dead man's voice,
>stammering, a little in the earth.*
>   from "For James Dean" by Frank O'Hara

Being chiseled from the rock was your undoing. Chips and dust
hung in sunlight, driftless, left a bitter taste on our tongues.
You wore movie titles like leather jackets with many zippers.

Racing is the only time you felt whole. Driving fast made drunk girls laugh,
tight corners, they'd fall on your lap with just a flash of your smile.
A giant, you died east of myth. You didn't see yourself crashing

as you were crashing. In slow motion. Will I find you in Fairmount, Indiana
where a man in black asked to trade his collar for your jacket? Will I find you
on the roadside at that blind intersection, a shadow cast by shadow?

At the crash site, I climbed into the wreck to pull you back. Your burnt skin
already turned to dirt, my own hands grasping the rasp and the hammer,
and only then do I remember, I remember, I remember you are no longer here.

Face on the Floor

When I lean over to pick up toys,
my notebook falls from my shirt.

Loose papers fan out
across the hardwood.

I see my son's face on a battlefield
in the pages on the floor.

You think I would learn,
but I have no other pockets.

When the loose pages scatter,
there is my son, face down.

I quickly pick up the papers,
and shuffle the whole mess back

into my breast pocket
fighting back the horrible image.

I return to picking up the house—
Legos, books, blocks, cars,

(my back grows stiff
picking up all this stuff);

thinking about dinner, the bills,
the war thirteen years from now.

GEORGE ESTREICH

Photo by Ellie Estreich

George and his wife moved to the Willamette Valley in September of 1998 when she accepted a job at Oregon State University. He had studied poetry writing at the University of Virginia with Charles Wright and Gregory Orr (BA, 1986), then received an MFA in poetry at Cornell (1989), where he studied with Robert Morgan and A.R. Ammons. He published one chapbook (*Elegy for Dan Rabinowitz*, 1993) and completed most of a full-length collection. Two of the poems included here, "Daughter, 4, Traces Newspaper" and "Codes," are Corvallis poems. Both were written, for the most part, at Noah's Bagels, where George used to take his older daughter, Ellie; they had an agreement that she would color for 30 minutes while he wrote. In the poems, he wound up writing about sitting in Noah's Bagels and writing while Ellie colored. The poems were first published in *Textbook Illustrations of the Human Body*, which won the Gorsline Prize from Cloudbank Books in 2003. The press's offices were across the street from Noah's Bagels. After the book came out, he read both locally (The Magic Barrel annual hunger benefit and the Corvallis-Benton County Library) and in the valley: Third Thursday Poets (Jackson's Books, Salem), Second Sunday Readings (Stayton), the Silverton Poetry Festival and the Windfall Reading Series at the Eugene Public Library. Most of his published writing since then has been prose nonfiction: *The Shape of the Eye* (SMU Press, 2011; Penguin, 2013; Oregon Book Award in Creative Nonfiction, 2012) and *Fables and Futures: Biotechnology, Disability, and the Stories We Tell Ourselves* (MIT Press, 2019; Oregon Book Award finalist; an NPR Best Science Book selection). He continues to write poems, one of which ("Written in the Air") is included here. Find out more about George at georgeestreich.com.

Acknowledgments. Written in the Air (*Underwater New York*); Daughter, 4, Traces Newspaper (*Textbook Illustrations of the Human Body*); Codes (*Textbook Illustrations of the Human Body*); Reasons for Building.

Written in the Air

And everything in the river was reassembled
into a shining plane that surfaced,
its wings dripping light, and headed west:
the giraffe rinsed clean of its spots,
skin, bones, and heart, immaculate
at last; the real cars and the toy cars and the parts
they became and what became
of the parts, a vast becoming,
axles freed of rotation, bones of position,
everything polished and dissociated and new,
above the city and heading west
like a visible vanishing point,
the torn edge of a wing trailing long silver threads,
the fat nacelles leaving no vapor trail,
only a long flume of altered clarity
like the glass in an old house
where the daylight moon wavers, then solidifies.
It is going west, with everything lost, it is heading home.
I would like to be aboard, but my heart is in the river.

Daughter, 4, Traces Newspaper

1.
She likes orange, pink, purple, green,
        so the words fluoresce,
    neon in fog:

           BUSH VICTORIOUS IN
           WASHINGTON, VIRGINIA

           FIRST GRADER SHOOTS CLASSMATE
           AS TEACHER, STUDENTS WATCH

        Now she is outlining

The Oregonian,
as if she were hollowing out
        each word,
or draining them
    to be refilled.
She doesn't look up. The ballpoint
follows each serif and curve.
      She works
like a prisoner on a tunnel,
turning her sentence
into a wavering line, a path
      through the thick dirt of the present.

What's this say? she asks.

2.

    Out here,
the landscape's homesick for the East:
        Albany, Salem, Portland.
    We're eating New York Bagels
at our usual table
        under a picture of the Brooklyn Bridge,
    next to the sugar packets and plastic stirrers,
our paper cups imprinted
    with a slick, personable, Yiddish-inflected pledge
of customer service,
      straight from the company's founder.
      I'm a bad copy myself,
      nth generation, my borders smudged, uncertain,
    New York blurred in me, Judaism all but invisible.

3.

She sets aside the headlines
    and turns to Northwest Living,
        unearthing the artifacts
        of a lost civilization,
            their contours bitten and worn,
        glowing as if a black
    light shone on them:

        Nike and Intel,
           the horoscope's twins, the dotted line
around a coupon, a percent sign
      from a one-day sale.
          Of the people,
hardly a trace remains:
      faces are skulls—
            she leaves the eyes empty—
and a candidate's reduced
      to the squiggle of a hairline.

      I don't recognize, at first,
           the irregular shape
in the center, the one
      the others crowd towards.
      Then I do:
      it's the mother and child
           from the front page, fused
into a single form,
      a human-shaped hole,
where a wash of light
      buried them, grain by grain.

4.
I trace "New Jersey" to read "Oregon."
I trace "suburb" and it comes out "town."
I trace "good schools" to read "good schools."
We like it here. We might stay.

5.
She turns to the weathermap:
      inside her west-moving
      line, the country seems a diagram
          of her parents' demographic,
a dispersed rainbow of degrees,
      a muddled covenant
           renewed daily with the chosen,
      the educated and mobile: a short-term
contract, temps predicted everywhere,

           precip over the tech writers
     migrating west, light flurries
              on software engineers and postdocs,
         adjuncts washed out
                  in heavy flooding.

Dad, she says, pointing to the watch.

6.
We move on, as our parents moved on.
                  We peel a skin of admonitions
                  from a heavy book:
    a cheat sheet, the minimum,
           light enough to travel.
           It's enough. It'll have to do.

7.
    Can I see? I say.
    Here, she says.

Under the rippled glaze
           of the tracing paper,
under its weightless crush
       of images and words,
    her fingerprints
           are clear, her palm
            a shadow far beneath,
so the sheet itself seems a depth
whose surface glitters, like a harbor,
      with the ruins of the city
          that rises above it,
    intact, shining.

Codes

> *Think of it as the highest form of writing, which in itself is the greatest invention of man. Be proud that you can record the language in its graceful, mysterious lines and curves. Aim constantly to acquire artistic skill in executing these lines and curves. You can, if you will, make the study of shorthand a perfect joy instead of a task.*
>
> John F. Gregg, "Hints and Helps for the Shorthand Student"

1.
It was hearts for awhile, nothing but hearts.
    Then it was houses, then stars.
    Then came writing,
        or "writing,"
          her wordless scrawl
on sheets torn from my notebook
            and passed across the table.

Dad. It's on the cardinal.
I look at the wall clock. I put my pencil down.

Dad. I wrote more than you.

2.
        Unreadable script
           for the day's rehearsals:

Coffee shop, Pacific Northwest. A window table.
A father, mid-thirties; a daughter, five.
They work without speaking.

She crosses a line out. The paper tears.

Your writing, my mother said. It looks like worm tracks. Like earthworms.
You should talk, I said.

Dad, says Ellie. *Is it five minutes?*

3.
                    Each space
            denotes a new word,
          which she murmurs
                        as she writes:
Then ... Dad ... said ... we ... could ... go.

4.
I scan the lines: words appear,
        sort of, *no* and *is*
        embedded like fossils
                        in the dense scribble:
                fragments textured
                and colored by the rock
        that pervades them,
as a sediment of the personal
                settles into the given
forms, into what
        we share and recognize.

There's lots of stories in there, she says.
Actually it's one big story. But it's too long to tell
all that, I don't remember what it says.

5.
Slash, quotation mark, backwards E:
                in a New Jersey suburb
                whose light I have misplaced,
                        my mother guided my hand
                briskly through the changed
                    syllables of my name,
                          in *katakana*,
                              the spiky alphabet invented,
                in the country she left,
                for foreign words:
JY-O-JI. She smiled.

                Now, she said. Your turn.

6.

    I found a stenographer's notebook
        in a North Carolina attic. Years ago.
            Virginia Couch penciled neatly on the cover.
              Under the single bulb
I paged through hours
        of shorthand practice,

a page of *l*, a page of *m*,
        a woman learning a code
            designed to erase her
                  almost completely,

like the flecks and dots
        of its minimal alphabet:
in the typed copy
        of the letter of understanding,
                she'd be reduced

            to a pair of initials,
a last word in the shadow
            of the next-to-last:
    XY:xx
like a parent standing over a child,
        dictating the terms
    and conditions, dependent
        clause, independent clause,

repeat after me: we continue
        through a deep transcription …

(Don't write, my mother said. Do something else.
And: Did you know? Hiroshi Oniki is with Goldman, Sachs.)

7.

        Page of *r*, page of *s* …
but towards the end
    the diary began,
        long, unparagraphed entries

under neatly Palmered dates.

The days whisper their dictation;
        we take it down.
        We encode and reproduce.
        We type up the minutes
                of another year,
transcribing the voices, in secret.
        We account for past losses,
                column by column;
        we finish the story.
                      This one ends with my mother writing
        her novel about the war.

8.

                I could hear her calling
from the kitchen. I was seven, maybe eight.
        Unfinished dialogue
                in the Smith-Corona,
        whole phrases blacked out
like a letter home
        from the front,
        pinholed and fragmented
                by the rat-a-tat x
held down, different from the humming
        silence and irregular
                stutter of invention.
    It "contained adult material." I'd read it when I was older.
I tried to see through the x's. I parsed
                the changes, uncomprehending.
        Between the lines were *kanji*
I could not read,
        though I understood them
        like a touch,
                her hand evident
in the flat unsentimental
        slashes of the ballpoint:
                they floated above circled nouns,
    superscripts to the footnote

                of her unreadable, other life,
        stray images of the understanding
                    whose graceful lines elude us,
          hovering like the dream
of our effort and smudged corrections.
    I left the room saying *What is it?*

9.

        A child is a witness.
            During the air raids, she told me,
      her father used to dance
      on the edge of the pit
          they'd dug in the yard,
            calling down to his family,
    saying, What difference will that make
          if a bomb falls on the house?

    I want your permission, I said, to tell that in a poem.
    You can tell this, she said, if you describe how the shelter really was. It was like the hole for a coffin, maybe six feet deep and three feet wide. There was a bamboo roof covered with dirt.

        Where was it in the yard?
        It was in the garden.

        Did your father ever go in the shelter?
        No, he never did.

10.

        She calls on my birthday.
        Are you writing? she asks.
        Her novel's filed
                with tax returns, passports, letters.

        As she taught me
           through the wall,
           tapping it out for years
                in what could've been
        one of two languages, but was

        only one,
it is happiness,
pure happiness, to write.

        But a life of writing
is not necessarily happy.

        Be careful, she says. Chores can interfere with your work.

        Our truest signatures
            are endless, and in code.

11.
Ellie returns to pictures. I'm relieved.
    This is a worm with polka dots
        in blue-and-green dirt.
    This is a girl under a rainbow,
fishing for bluegills.
Then one day she wants to sound out *am*.
The labor of it,
        saying *aaaa ... aaaa ... A!*
        Then *mmm ...*

        So I too alternate
            between an ease as meaningless
                as it is fluent,
        and the ache of the exact
        intention, the single word.

Under the coffee, it smells like fall.

12.
    She points to two squiggles
        in the middle of the page:
That says "The End."

Reasons for Building

```
                            A
                          child
                        could see
                      it In the sun
                    the sloping lines
                  of the roof and under
                moonlight the lit windows
              and figures moving inside the
            shadow And I liked the blueprints
          where the house in its east elevation
        floated against a dark ground an incision
      in twilight I wanted to construct an image of
    home I wanted a selfportrait in wood and wire and
  concrete A version of the body that soft clock I bear
  from place to place The mismatched gears of its heart
    and lungs the coiled mainspring of its code the
    restlessness of its perpetual movement I wanted
    a place fixed against motion an absence defined
    against the intricate Sunlit rooms to stop time
    I wanted        that it be        mine not
    in title        alone that        dwelling
    of paper        but by the        labor of
    hands in        deed For a        house is
    a vision        descending        into the
    paradise        of details        settling
    itself in place A weighted image Something seen
    through So I marked off a site with string then
    began to dig And it seemed like archaeology The
    brick fragments Coke cans wisps of insulation a
    nail halfburied in clay and the house unearthed
    day by day in the slow reconstruction of a life
    I stayed        there even        before I
    was done        lying each        night on
    my floor        looking up        at stars
    a map of        the undone        drifting
    overhead        divided by        darkened
    beams It        seemed the        negative
    of a house of light an image      reversed
    I thought form was permanent      and that
    measure was the soul of form      the line
    leveled against the world Sleeping like a child
    I dreamed thirty seconds of an inch beneath the
exploded diagram of my life those lit ruins sinking each night into the earth and rising as a single star
```

Words of Healing
Words of Hope

First Sunday at Four Performance

in
Poetry and Music

Sunday, March 2
4 p.m.

Good Samaritan Regional Medical Center
Murray Memorial Library

Featured artists:

- Steven Sher - poet and author of 10 books, including Traveler's Advisory, an Oregon Book Awards finalist
- Linda Gelbrich – poet, instructor, therapist and integrative healthcare facilitator at Heartspring Wellness Center
- Wendi Chambers - musician on guitar and vocals, transcriptionist for Good Samaritan Regional Medical Center

Presented by: the Willamette Literary Guild in cooperation with Good Samaritan Regional Medical Center, the Arts in Medicine Program of Samaritan Integrative Medicine and ArtCentric.

World AIDS Day 2002

An Afternoon of Music and Poetry

December 1, 2002
2:00 p.m.—5:00 p.m.
Corvallis Public Library

ending stigma and discrimination

poetic license

reading and reception

**Saturday, April 8, 7—9 p.m.
Corvallis Arts Center**
700 SW Madison

Announcing the publication of ***poetic license***, the first chapbook by the poetry group, poetic license

You are invited to a reading by:
Pam Wilson
Linda Varsell Smith
Cindy Smith
Susan Shumway
Wyn Schoch
Carol Ann Lantz
Linda Gelbrich
Jesse Ford

Cover art from a pointing by William E. Shumway

LINDA GELBRICH

Photo courtesy of the poet

Linda Gelbrich (aka Linda Williamson) is a "native Oregonian" who has lived in Central and Western Oregon. She has resided in Corvallis for the past 50 years. Oregon's outdoors and the landscape of the Southwest continue to influence her and find their way into many of her poems. She has degrees from Oregon colleges, taught at Linn-Benton Community College and for most of her working career was a medical Clinical Social Worker at Good Samaritan Hospital and in their Integrative Medicine Program. She worked as a therapist, group facilitator and adult educator, and encouraged writing, relaxation and being outdoors as part of mind-body-spirit health. She occasionally led workshops on writing for health. Linda's poems have appeared in numerous anthologies and journals, and on note cards with photographs (in collaboration with her husband Keith). The note cards have been carried by Grass Roots Books and Music in Corvallis since 2010. One of her poems is part of a permanent art installation in Corvallis and another was featured on a theater marquee. She has produced many chapbooks of poetry, and her writing is included in two books of daily spiritual reflections published by *Forward Movement*. She coordinated or assisted in organizing literary events for many years, including the annual William Stafford celebrations in Corvallis beginning in 2004, encouraging collaboration with other organizations and businesses. She served on the Board of Trustees for the Friends of William Stafford, and was recognized for her efforts to keep writers informed of literary events around the state. Benton County Cultural Trust presented her with an "Outstanding Contribution to Humanities" award. She is one of the Poetic License poets, is involved with Marys Peak Poets and writes weekly with a small group of friends.

Acknowledgments. Watching a Wasp the Day after John Lewis's Funeral (*New Verse News; pan/dem/ick 2020: An Anthology of Pandemic Poems*, Oregon Poetry Association); Summer Sounds in the Neighborhood (*Poetic License*); Brittle (*Poetic License*); Along a Trail at Shotpouch Creek (*To Topos: Poetry International*); Listen to the River (*River Songs*, Willamette River Diptych).

Watching a Wasp the Day after John Lewis's Funeral

A small yellowjacket joins me
at the patio table this morning,
absorbed in the pinch of sausage
I set aside on the tablecloth
a short distance away.

It wraps its body
halfway around the morsel,
its legs and jaw clamped on,
and the sausage begins to roll
toward the table edge.
I stop the rolling with my notebook.
The wasp hangs on.

The second time it rolls to the edge
both fall to the deck,
and the wasp hangs on
until it bites off a small piece,
flies away, then returns for more.

All this happens
while I finish breakfast,
get out my pen and begin to write,
wondering if I, too, could be
so absorbed in anything
that I'd keep on with my work
no matter who or what
sat near me,

no matter the rolling and falling
that surely would happen,
that I'd keep on, even
if bruised and battered,
that I'd want something so much
I could not be deterred,
would not give up,
as long
as I still
had breath.

Summer Sounds in the Neighborhood

Outside I hear
neighbors talking,
cars humming up and down
the street, hammers striking nails,
a lawn mower's cough and growl,
the rhythmic crack and thud
of wood being stacked.

After workers put away their tools,
we hear the papery voices
of dry leaves, a robin's song,
chickadees, the buzzy drone
of hummingbird wings,

and more subtle still
is the sun's golden song,
the tap of ants' feet, hum
of warm stone, and even sounds
my body makes
while slowly sinking
into a patio chair.

Brittle

In these last days of summer
stems of dahlias break
with the slightest nudge
or wisp of breeze.
Rhododendron's dry leaves slough off
and begin to pile in drifts
along the sidewalk. Some flowers
still shout their colors, while others
begin to shrink into themselves.

Oak leaves thin now, their soft green
fading to speckled and brown,
edges crisp and dry. Soon a wind

will charge through the yard
and crack fine branches from oaks,
ripping leaves loose to fly and fall.

My grief, as autumn approaches,
is not just about summer's withering
beauty. My dad died long ago
in November. Years later my mom's health
declined in autumn, leading toward
her winter's death. One October I fell
from a ladder onto the deck.
Bones broke.
It is a brittle time.

Along a Trail at Shotpouch Creek

It feels like home here where limbs bow
and arch in the coolness of shade,
where they lean across the path
and caress one another. I hear a long sigh
of the hot breeze as it rocks
a spider's finely-crafted cup of silver filament.

Filtered sun spills gold through
this community of alder, maple and fir,
and moss is growing thick on surfaces
along the creek. Everything

is at home here, even the sword fern
that grows from the top of an old stump
and drapes over the sides, comfortable
as uncombed hair.

I step with care on this tended path that winds
and dips toward the free-running creek.
Birds continue to sing and chat as I pass by.
When a place feels so much like home
you could walk and walk and never be truly lost.

Listen to the River

Don't believe anyone who tells you
rivers have no time for stories.
Don't trust anyone who says
They're just hell-bent for the sea.

Listen to the river in the quiet of the evening
after the heron has gone to roost.
Put your ear to the water and
listen with your skin
to whispers, roarings and ripples.

She tells of children and wet, stick-mouthed dogs,
of lovers exchanging river-side promises
while drawing dreams in silt with their toes,
of those who fish for solitude and inspiration,
of men whose way back home got lost
and now sleep along her banks.

She tells of icy mountain lakes
that wake when rainbow trout sneak back
after chasing flies among morning stars,
of lakes sending out their dreams that flow
through snow and fir to wake the valley.

You'll hear of cedar strip canoes, slap-tail beavers
and flocks of egrets rising
like dense white mist in back water places.
Then she'll boast and roar of swirling madness
and the way she moves the mountains.

Even though you stoop to hear and watch the eddy swirl
she slips her ancient, watery fingers
into fields and forest,
churns up stories and floats them over
to those who wait along the shore.

CHARLES GOODRICH

Photo courtesy of the poet

After growing up and going to college in the Midwest, Charles moved to Oregon in 1974. On the day that he arrived by bus in Portland, there was a big festival in progress—tens of thousands of people dancing to live music on the riverfront. He learned that the city had closed a highway and converted it into Tom McCall Riverfront Park. They were closing roads to create parks—how thrilling! He became an Oregonian on the spot, finding work as a groundskeeper at Marylhurst Convent. For the next two-plus decades, he supported his poetry writing habit by working as a professional gardener. When Charles moved to Corvallis in 1980, he got a job as the groundskeeper for the Children's Farm Home, then became the first supervisor of the Benton County Corrections Work Crew, and subsequently the master gardener for the Benton County Courthouse. During that time, he and his wife Kapa built their own house in southtown Corvallis, near the confluence of the Marys and Willamette Rivers, where they raised their son Elliot. During the 1990s, literary events around town were frequent and lively. Charles was among a group who founded the Willamette Literary Guild, hosting readings at the Corvallis Arts Center and other venues. He was also a regular participant in a poetry critique group that met at Dale Willey's house, where many of the writers in this anthology tried out their poems. By the end of the millennium, he had worn out his knees working as a gardener, so he enrolled in the Creative Writing program at Oregon State University and earned his MFA in 2001. Subsequently, until his retirement in 2017, he served as director of the Spring Creek Project for Ideas, Nature, and the Written Word at OSU, a program that brings together creative writers, artists, environmental philosophers and environmental scientists to re-imagine our relationship to nature. His gardening and home-building exploits are chronicled in a collection of essays, *The Practice of Home: Biography of a House* (Lyons Press), and in four volumes of poetry: *Insects of South Corvallis* (Cloudbank Books); *Going to Seed: Dispatches from the Garden* (Silverfish Review Press); *A Scripture of Crows* (Silverfish Review Press); and *Watering the Rhubarb* (Flowstone Press). Charles also co-edited the volumes *In the Blast Zone: Catastrophe and Renewal on Mount St. Helens* and *Forest under Story: Creative Inquiry in an Old-Growth Forest*. His poems and essays have appeared in *Orion, High Country News, The Sun* and many other journals and anthologies. Find out more about Charles at charlesgoodrich.com.

Acknowledgments. A Lecture on Aphids (*Insects of South Corvallis*); Vacuuming Spiders (*Insects of South Corvallis*); Why We Do It (*Insects of South Corvallis*); Interstition (*Going to Seed: Dispatches from the Garden*); Wild Geese (*Going to Seed: Dispatches from the Garden*).

A Lecture on Aphids

She plucks my sleeve.
"Young man," she says, "you need to spray.
You have aphids on your roses."

In a dark serge coat and a pill-box hat
by god it's my third-grade Sunday-school teacher,
shrunken but still stern, the town's
most successful corporate attorney's mother.
She doesn't remember me. I holster
my secateurs, smile publicly,
and reply, Ma'am,

did you know a female aphid is born
carrying fertile eggs? Come look.
There may be five or six generations
cheek by jowl on this "Peace" bud.
Don't they remind you
of refugees
crowding the deck of a tramp steamer?
Look through my hand lens—
they're translucent. You can see their dark innards
like kidneys in aspic.

Yes, ma'am, they are full-time inebriates,
and unashamed of their nakedness.
But isn't there something wild and uplifting
about their complete indifference to the human prospect?

And then I do something wicked. Ma'am, I say,
I love aphids! And I squeeze
a few dozen from the nearest bud
and eat them.

After the old woman scuttles away
I feel ill
and sit down to consider
what comes next. You see,

aphids
aren't sweet
as I had always imagined.
Even though rose wine is their only food,
aphids
are bitter.

Vacuuming Spiders

I admire their geometrical patience,
the tidy way they wrap up leftovers,
their willingness to be the earth's
most diligent consumers of small bitternesses.

Sometimes at night I hear them
casting silk threads, clicking their spinnerets,
plucking their webs like blind Irish harpists.
I can almost taste the fruit of the fly
like sucking the pulp from a grape.

But when their webs on the ceiling
begin to converge, and the floor
glitters with shards of insect wings
I drag out the vacuum
and poke its terrible snout under the sofa,
behind the radio—everywhere,

for this is the home of a human being
and I must act like one
or the whole picture goes haywire.

Why We Do It

      for Clem Starck

1.
You got your old farmhouse nearly restored
before you relapsed into writing poetry.
Since my last visit
you've hammered the language
for a few scant stanzas,
while the door to your study remains unhung,
the empty drawerholes in the kitchen cabinets gape,
and the gangplank sags
where your front porch steps
are still not built.

In the guest room, between bare studs
you've stacked up hundreds of books
in half a dozen languages, to insulate
your old age against boredom.

Your children have grown up and left home,
believing perhaps
that all fathers hole up nightly in the pumphouse,
and write things
oddly-shaped
and slow-growing as the old oaks
that loomed at their bedroom windows
and creaked spookily in the night.

2.
Past midnight
the books we've pulled
to praise or to curse, to read aloud
under your gooseneck lamp,
lie piled on the floor
deep as manure.

Hoarse, a little drunk,
we argue all the louder,
skewering murky images,

deflating overblown phrases
as if our vehemence alone
could rescue a poem from its own obscurities.

But finally we start to fade.
I think of my wife, at home
in bed.

Through the open window, a bat
zigzags into the study,
flutters around us,
then dangles from a bookshelf
head downward, eyes wide,
ears pricked.

Having an audience
revives us.

3.
Overdosed, at last, on verse
we walk to my truck, reciting
our backlog of autumn chores: cut firewood,
mend fence, gravel the driveway,
insulate pipes …

Jobs, family, debts—
our days are full enough
without the nagging compulsion to write.

"Why do we do it?" the beleaguered
carpenter-poet asks his friend the gardener-poet
somewhere in darkest rural Oregon.

We shake hands,
shake heads, retell
one last story, the earliest light
just seeping over the ridge.

Interstition

Sticking to ritual makes things tick. Ask the robin sitting her nest. Ask the lilacs beginning to bud. Ask me. Or better yet, take this shovel and help me plant these spuds. You dig the trench and I'll set a seed potato every two feet in the row.

Because it's St. Patrick's Day, and that's when we plant potatoes. The college boys down the street are celebrating another way, playing ping pong in their driveway puking drunk, because they know as well as you and I do that famine is just one blight away. While they put their faith in cheap revelry, I'm paying court to the old dirt gods, burying these spuds with a prayer they'll let me stay another year above-ground.

You might think it's superstition, but it's actually *inter*stition, acting on blind faith that the individual things we see are all stitched together by something potent and invisible. Better not ask what it is. Just dig.

Wild Geese

I'm picking beans when the geese fly over, Blue Lake pole beans I figure to blanch and freeze. Maybe pickle some dilly beans. And there will be more beans to give to the neighbors, forcibly if necessary.

The geese come over so low I can hear their wings creak, can see their tail feathers making fine adjustments. They slip-stream along so gracefully, riding on each other's wind, surfing the sky. Maybe after the harvest I'll head south. Somebody told me Puerto Vallarta is nice. I'd be happy with a cheap room. Rice and beans at every meal. Swim a little, lay on the beach.

Who are you kidding, Charles? You don't like to leave home in the winter. Spring, fall, or summer either. True. But I do love to watch those wild geese fly over, feel these impertinent desires glide through me. Then get back to work.

Marys Peak
Sentinel of the Coast Range

Photography and Poetry

Exhibit Catalog
published by the
Willamette Valley PhotoArts Guild
and the
Marys Peak Group of the Sierra Club

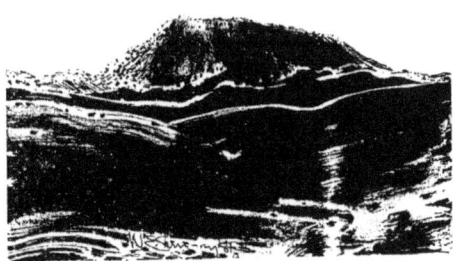

Tcha teemanwi:
Poems for Marys Peak

edited by
Charles Goodrich
Michael Spring

DONNA HENDERSON

Photo by Joy Reyneke

Born in Portland, Donna has lived much of her life in the Mid-Willamette Valley, with the exception of some years on the East Coast, in the Middle East and in France. In 1986, she and her husband, Rick Sutliff, moved from Salem to a 20-acre pasture-and-timber property near Kings Valley, where they lived for the next 25 years and restored the oak savannah hidden under the overgrown fir plantation, also planting 2,000 wetland trees in the riparian zone of the old pasture through which Fuller Creek runs. It was in the midst of all that spacious, leafy beauty that she really began to be able to practice poetry as a way of deeply seeing and feeling. Airlie Press was birthed there in 2007 (with Jessica Lamb, Anita Sullivan and Carter McKenzie). In 2007, *The Eddy Fence*, one of the first two poetry collections published by Airlie Press, was an Oregon Book Award finalist. Donna's poetry has been anthologized in *Alive at the Center: Contemporary Poems from the Pacific Northwest*; *Writing Our Watershed*, edited by Gail Oberst (Luckiamute Watershed Council, 2008); and *A Fierce Brightness: Twenty-five Years of Women's Poetry* (CALYX Press, 2002). Her chapbook *Transparent Woman* (Howlet Press, 1996) was an Oregon Book Award finalist. Her poems, essays, reviews and song lyrics have appeared in a variety of magazines such as *Rattle, CALYX Journal, American Letters and Commentary, The Harvard Review, Writers Forum, Fireweed, Cutbank* and *Gold Man Review*. She has served in *CALYX Journal*'s editorial collective and as an editor of *Fireweed*; established *Wild Women Recite!*, an Independence, OR, reading series featuring women writers; taught craft of poetry at Willamette University; and received a writing residency in 2019 at Playa, on Summer Lake, possibly her favorite spot on the planet. *Send Word* is her recently-completed new collection of poems. Donna is a Licensed Clinical Social Worker and holds an MFA from Warren Wilson College. She presently lives in Maupin, OR. Find out more about Donna at donnacatehenderson.com.

Acknowledgments. Transparent Woman (*CALYX Journal*; *A Fierce Brightness: Twenty-five Years of Women's Poetry*, CALYX Press; *Transparent Woman*, Howlet Press); Lunar (*Send Word*, Riparian Press); First Ice (*The Eddy Fence; Alive at the Center: Contemporary Poems from the Pacific Northwest*); Between Sleeping and Waking (*Send Word*, Riparian Press); The Sanctuary (*The Eddy Fence*).

Transparent Woman

I've rushed down past the churning
bees in their glass-cased hive to be here on time,
passing the boxes of pettable chicks,
the pendulum, fossils, past the fiberglass
heart huge as my playhouse (well,
                                  rushing through),

to arrive as this holy light wobbles up
from its stage-side canisters and the music starts,
soothing and scientific, & the drape lifts
off by the usual invisible means &
                                She appears,

        in the basement of the science museum,
half-lit, naked and marvelous with her perfect
posture, lucite arms straight and slightly apart,
palms turned toward us like the Blessed Virgin's,
helplessly welcoming.

And in that voice
sibilant & disembodied as a stewardess'
She begins as I know she will:

       I ...
       am the Transparent Woman.

... and I am thrilled again; I don't know
how many times I've come but it's good as
new, especially that first   "*I ... am*"
as she begins to describe herself,
organ by organ:

       This ... is my brain

the voice flows as her skull lights—*bing!*—
clear tubes coiled behind her Jackie Kennedy
flip of clear hair—

and her disinterest
rivets me as much as her parts themselves:
she demonstrates them like seat belts—no pride,
no shame, no special affections—she just
goes on, with that detachment,
revealing –

    These ... are my breasts She intones,
and they flash on—*bing!*—like headlights,
pale green veins and glands threading out from the nipples
                  as our giggles start ...
                                    and I want her to stop it now;

she is immune to shame but I'm embarrassed
for her. It's too much:
the kids laughing,
me laughing with them,
my small self already divided—

      This ... is my heart ...
            ... my womb ...
            ... my intestines ...

and with
      ... my skin, which is an organ too ...
She is all transparent, done

before our ridicule, awe,
    —they're all the same to her—
Her entire job to fill with light
before us, over and over ...

I don't know anyone like her.

Lunar

      for SL and MJ

Diving into the zone of transition
said Sue across the room (or something like that).

Early morning lumenumbra of the playa's planes.

Many were sleepy from the early a.m.
display which had proceeded without my gaze.

Then Marilyn invited me to her table
of alchemy, where we beeswaxed yesterday's
sunrise sketch (mine) and made it glow.

And I marveled at the way the wax both married
and clarified: lost lines reestablished their statements,
and the frantic furze of the pastel parts … relaxed.

Lumenumbra.
Zone of the unknown

transition. The playa's
sleepy planes.

The moon had proceeded without my gaze!

Watchers said the wonder was the way
the Milky Way was visible along with the moonglow.

I supposed it emboldened Sue, who
traipsed out onto the muckscape then

promptly fell into the playa's planes.

From which tumble into the umbra she eventually
emerged, face coated with moonglow,
wrap spattered with milky clay.

First Ice

We wake up as the darkness begins
giving way, first to an indigo

glow like laundry bluing,
phosphorescent and implausibly dense.

Shades of trees appear, then trees,
then a dreamy, scintillant

stillness unfurls as light, as landscape
under a spell. A fat sleekness

blisters and thickens the porch; in the pasture
grass blades bow down in glass sleeves.

The woods are themselves and not
themselves in their subtle glister,

the way a truly glamorous woman,
my grandmother used to say (charm bracelets rustling),

conceals every seam and trace
of her artifice, leaving pure effect.

Inside, a chef on T.V. makes aspic
while we wait for the forecast.

*One strives for the clearest, thinnest
gel*, he is saying; *one wants to illuminate*

one's terrine, not to thicken it!
And as he spreads his glaze, I see the soul

rise from its loaf and lay its glossy
immaterial bliss across that surface of meat &

salt with its scallion *fleur-de-lis*,
making it marvelous.

As the world is, today—as it was
in the beginning, that last instant

water, matter and light were one,
each distinct, not yet separate.

Between Sleeping and Waking

were bells on a wet day, grey
panes of puddles a pool in a well.
Blame far away, a flame
covered or even snuffed.
Rough crusts of ice on grass
crass calls of geese,
sheep fleece clotted with crud,
thud of some storm-tipped trees
breezes flexing their limbs, slim
shoots of early spring corms
through soil, roil of lambs in the field,
peeled trunks of antler-rubbed willows
their white-gold glow. The slow
flood in the swale, bales piled
high inside sheds, rosehips
redly festooning the sides of roads.
Rust on the mailbox, rocks braking
the race of the stream, the clock
breaking the space of dream—

The Sanctuary

It was late when I walked up the gravel
road to the clear-cut hill. Loggers gone
for the day, feller-buncher machines all still,
their claws and blades cooling.
A low sun laid its thick light on the slope,
the light sieved through the last, lean stand.
Into those wrecked woods I walked,
straight to the center pile,
laid myself down on a log
and apologized for my species.

I apologized to those trees for my species
with tears, but not without greed:
I wanted a word in turn.
Of forgiveness, reassurance,
I don't know—I wanted a word.
Which didn't come.
And what was I thinking, wanting more?
The trees, after all, were dead.

The trees were dead—only the light was there;
which I saw (as I stood between the machines
and their gruesome business, amid the piles and vines)
coated the whole sorry mess of us all,
without chastisement or preference.

Without chastisement or preference, the light
left, and I walked back down that road
and up my own, home to a solitude I was
bereft of now, sullied as it was.
Woke the next day to watch, over again,
one fir after another lean to the left
and fall, keening and cracking (*Screamers,*
the painter Emily Carr had called them:
final splinters that shriek as the trunk is torn).
For so long—oh, *forever*—I had counted on the forest's
persistence there, its green and cool surround.

Not to escape the sufferings of the world:
from which to bear them.

Now the violence was taking the forest too,
while I stood on my cedar deck,
inconsolable, seeing unceasingly.

Inconsolable, seeing unceasingly
a word arrived through the wound—
This is what it is to bear witness,
I saw inside. As the woods got small
the heart had to grow larger. To become,
by its breaking, what those woods had been.
Spacious, the heart would have to become,
and huge. Enough to hold all the trees
and their absence, and every other thing.

Mistry Guild
the true oracle of poetry & Art
Volume 1

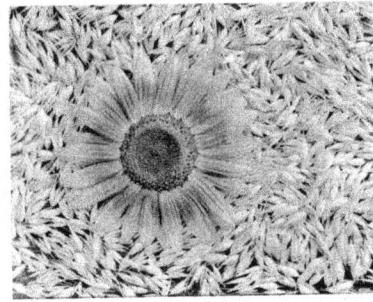

Featuring poetry, art, & photography from local
& national poets & artists

$8.95

FIREWEED
Poetry of Western Oregon

**Volume Six, Number Two
Winter 1995 $2.50**

BE DAVISON HERRERA

Photo courtesy of Betu Herrera Case

Be was born in Virginia in 1942. Before moving to Corvallis in the early 2000s, she was a community worker, a member of the Sacramento International Poetry Hall of Fame, the founder of the Shriners Hospitals Poetry and Pride Program, and part of the Inclusionists, a group of Sacramento poets and artists, and 100,000 Poets for Change. In Corvallis, she continued to teach poetry to developmentally challenged adults. Her joy was often in encouraging and promoting others. Be's poems have appeared in 19 anthologies including the *Nevada County Poetry Series Year 2001 Anthology*; *Poets Ponder Photographs*; *Voices of the New Sun* (Escritores del Nuevo Sol, 2004); *Flowers of Love* (Vietnamese Poetry Society, vols. 2000, 2002 and 2004); and *The Other Side of Yesterday* (poetry and illustrations, Circle of Friends annual reading, Sacramento, 2006). A book of her poems, *Love Songs*, was published by The Vietnamese International Poetry Society in 2007. She was an associate editor for VIPS Press, which published in English, French and Vietnamese. She is also the author of seven chapbooks and was co-author of *Alice Fong: A Retrospective*. As a performance poet, visual artist and sculptor, she created portable (mostly) labyrinths (and led workshops) around the US and internationally. She has performed her poems across the US (e.g., California Stage-Wilkerson Theatre, Sacramento), in Paris and Amsterdam. Be also taught for six years at the University of California, Davis. Her sculpture has been exhibited in the US, Canada, Mexico, El Salvador, France, China (PRC), Italy, India (Bengal) and Egypt. In Corvallis, Be organized readings featuring the cognitively challenged adults that she worked with in poetry and visual arts. She volunteered until she could no longer manage it due to her own cognitive decline; she is now in a memory care facility. Be also organized displays of local writers' works at the Corvallis Public Library. As an editor, she worked with Frances Stilwell on a book of native plants of Oregon featuring Frances's pastels.

Acknowledgments. A Blues Song (*Vietnamese International Poetry Society*); I Might Enjoy Being Wordless; Meditations on the Song Celestia (*The Other Side of Yesterday*); Talk to Me ... I Will Listen (included in a word performance at California Stage-Wilkerson Theatre, May 28, 2009, Sacramento, CA); Cold Food Day. (All these poems were selected by Linda Gelbrich and Betu Herrera Case.)

A Blues Song

If you want it
the doctor will open
if you want it

The door will open
into sunshine and window
to mark a daily passage
into sunshine and shadow

To mark a daily passage
in the absence of tolerance
      or
         pain
To mark a daily passage
if you want it.

I Might Enjoy Being Wordless

but not yet

so now I am wordless
   dry interiorly without written conceits
so much dread
mixed with delight

of facts new to me
   like whale origins
on land switched from cows
   to oceanic domiciles
every year some amazing fact
   enters my lexicon

birds changing course yearly on
   the same day

neither metaphors nor brilliant similes
   engage my attention

while rooting around natural miracles
   lists keep me
engaged in artful poesy practice
   but my mind
misses the music of poetics
   stranded by information
so rich   so instantly imaginable
   yet scarcely fathomable
who can measure such possibilities
  on a planet
red in tooth and claw

Meditations on the Song Celestial

   I ask what causes
      winds to blow
to caress lover's hand
        clasped
 what fierce fires are
championed by healthy
         egos
  can a child continue
dreaming after innocence
    is
   lost?
  who makes all parts
work synchronistically
   like an orchestra
   like a many petaled wildflower
   like the cycle of stones
      falling from mountain heights
         rolling mile on mile down
            to welcoming waters at a

    continent's edge
        then down down through the
        deep ocean's canyons
        to its floor there to rest
        safely until the geologic
        urges of stars beckon and
the great slabs upthrust beyond
            imagining
to create new land-locked
guardians with those same
stones welded together by
those same ancient fierce fires
returned to wind-blown heights
to begin their cyclic travels
        all over again
    are they the spark
    from a human eye
    born to freedom or
        winds bearing
        multiverses
    waiting to be born?

Talk to Me ... I will Listen

  walk with me
sounds spring between us
        talk with me
our feet will echo our mouths

shall I write to you in wingdings
or speak as our tongues siphon sound
  the drumheads of our every step

your sounds slide between my ribs
  like blood explores arteries

your sounds savor
        my bones' boundaries

    move your mouth at me
      sound can slip-slide
           between us
             I will catch it
   like a ball of light

Cold Food Day

        how to remember
some whose lives spread kindly
        habits of love

a Chinese seer embodied Confucius'
        teachings of respect
by protecting his elderly mother

        hid her away
in a secluded mountain cave
        but fire sped

sweeping through their high refuge
        it slaughtered both
leaders who remembered that saint

        chose to respect
his practices by proclaiming annually
        a fireless day
all eat only cold food

KAREN HOLMBERG

Photo courtesy of the poet

Karen was raised on the East Coast on a brackish cove off the Thames River, which feeds into Long Island Sound. Her father, a high school biology teacher, nurtured in her a love of biology and ecology, and her mother also fostered a love of nature, gardening and the plant world. Though still connected to her Atlantic roots, she has become a deep-rooted transplant to the Pacific Northwest, and her writing reflects this; the settings and cast of characters have grown increasingly Oregonian. Karen teaches in the MFA program at Oregon State University, where she also maintains a letterpress studio as a laboratory of the page where she and her students play with language as both text and visual image. The Shotpouch Cabin and its surrounding woods, part of the Spring Creek Project at OSU, provided the encounters with nettles and slugs, hatchlings and nurserymen memorialized in her poems. Karen's daughters Ava and Lily (thoroughgoing Oregonians) and their explorations of our breathtaking natural environment are her most potent inspirations. Her first book, *The Perseids*, won the Vassar Miller Prize and was published by the University of North Texas Press (2001); her second book, *Axis Mundi*, won the John Ciardi Prize and was published by BkMk Press (2013). *Slate Magazine* named *Axis Mundi* one of the ten best poetry titles of 2013. Individual poems have appeared in such magazines as *The Paris Review, Quarterly West, Slate, The Nation, Cimarron Review, Southern Poetry Review, Cave Wall, Nimrod, Subtropics*, and have won her a Discovery/The Nation Award. Her creative nonfiction has appeared in *Black Warrior Review, New England Review* and *Indiana Review*; two of her essays have been cited as Notable Essays in *Best American Essays* (2012 and 2013). Karen holds an MA in Slavic Languages and Literatures from the University of Southern California, an MFA in poetry from the University of California-Irvine and a PhD in English and Creative Writing from the University of Missouri. Her current writing project is a lyric novella/hybrid work based on a family history of emigration and orchard keeping.

Acknowledgments. The Slug (*Hunger Mountain*); Exchange of Azalea and Quail *(Terrain)*; To the Ox Netsuke in the Flea Market (*Terrain*); Surrogate (*West Branch*); Sweetbriar (*Comstock Review*). (All these poems appeared in *Axis Mundi*, BkMk Press.)

The Slug

      It glides by
with the grand leisure of a whale
in migration. Yet once it sees me
      it retires, melts a little
           foreskin over

      its face. The prompt
eyes probe upward and re-bloom, dewed
with humectants. I stroke its neck,
      glandular and chilled
           as a dog's nose.

      When I cover
the single nostril like a fife's
finger hole, the back contracts to buck
      me off in slo-mo.
           Or is time

      lapsing radically
when, under its mantle, tectonic
plates collide, a seam heightens, gains
      flute and pucker—and anon
           subsides, thumbed down

      by fleet
millennia as I gaze. It's young
again, the oldest young thing
      I know. A working proof
           of the axiom

      of nerdy cool:
that patterns purposely chosen
to clash can at times define
      what's dapper. So spots
           blurred like black

        galaxies enhance
the crisp effect of its mushroom-gill
pinstriped tableskirt. A train
        of glycerin lace tows
                a collection

        of debris;
chips of black basalt, the beige bells
of some mountain flower. What if, cooling
        as a cloud,
                a larger I

        pores over
my moraine (the things hitched up
to the bumper of my car,
        the ball-and-chains
                healed into me)—?

.
I pray I amuse It.

Exchange of Azalea and Quail

        Something special you're wanting?

        I'd a vision of a white azalea,
a crown to hover
        like a spreading oak's above the mound
I'd made, around which curved
        a bark path's rustic valley.

                Aye, true dwarf,
though that don't keep
        the bobwhite quail setting
her clutch beneath it.

        Size and heat
of shooter marbles left in the sun.

   Don't never see the mother go,
but she's always off the nest
   when he comes down the row.

Now, yesterday he felt nothing
   but a bit of shell. So he stepped
full weight on the shovel, leaned back
   to rock the root ball free, when up
boiled the shrub like a pan of milk, the chicks
   a clump he could've picked up
all at once.

   Ball of cockleburs
they was.

   Minute he got a finger on
they burst apart, tunneled
   like voles in the tall grass,

said the nurseryman, the boyish shock
   of tawny-silver bangs falling
across one candid eye as he set
   my azalea in the trunk.

To the Ox Netsuke in the Flea Market

You captured light, keeping some,
letting some go, alive as cartilage.
The hand the idea of you amused
fused porcine to bovine, ovine
to piscine, capping the gadfly-
maddened tossing head
with a snout's wooden spool,
planting a horn meek
as a sheep's teat inside each ear's
ragged cabbage leaf, dangling
a dewlap of earlobe dough
off a neck slick as a fingerling trout.

If I had held you shell-like to my ear
I might have caught
your maker's rumination:
commiseration whispering with delight.
Instead, I fell for you,
one of the many pettiness detectors
that booby-trap our world.
For the cloven toes on your left hind hoof
had fractured off, and the face
those absent noses left
was coarse as emery. That's all it took
to make me put you down, to
disenamor me.
To keep me from being
the better person who took you home.

Surrogate

*It fell—it fell from the sky—the nest—*they
crow, they clamor hoarsely. My older girl unfurls
her fist, reveals an egg the same faint blue
of the day moon, dull as frost and flawless
as a Jordan almond. Then holds the cell
to her shell of ear. *I think I hear it cry.*

In the pure parabola, a tented fracture,
then a flap thrown back, hinged with milky skin.
A cheep, subtle as a walled-up cricket's.
Something strains and shifts, chiseling out that peephole.
Slow-motion-sick, we watch as it revolves and winds
itself in kinked, yolk-stiffened down.

Stranded on the heating pad, all day it croons
a podcast of progress to the brooding Beyond.
The girl attunes her ear to it, becomes
its mother, hovering all day to watch the puncture
widen to an aperture in cloud-cover
over an empurpled, wrinkled continent.

Nothing simpler or more terrible: the head
jigging on a spring, the beak exploding
at a touch like a touch-me-not seedpod.
The metallic chirp chills our hearts like a notice
of default, or the mayday of the run-down
battery in the attic smoke alarm.

On its grin, a smear of blood where my tweezers
nicked the yellow bumpers. By noon
a scrotum of flies and wormlings dangled
off its breast. The eyes were blueberries
sealed in phyllo. The stubby wings
were livid pink and cocked like fetal thumbs.

I tried to emulate the mother's brisk de-winging
and de-songing: the plucking off of parts too crisp
or sharp. But the playground bully's song came back—*baldy,
baldy*—pure tenor notes mocking the sockets where
the matador capes and thighs attached. The stoic
oval stare came back: I held a paraplegic in my palm.

My daughters grieve as we return the hatchling
to the alley, setting the willow basket down
under the gorgon tree, the capped crux of black sheathed
power cables traveling down a galvanized spine
to enter New Morning Bakery. *We deliver fear
of failure fresh daily*, the brash world avows.

We back away. Above, the reedy feeding calls;
below, a sharp single-minded beacon. Something
flutter-tumbles like a clod of dust, refines to a swoop:
the sparrow perches, runs some feathers through her beak
to zip them tight. She cocks her head, sedately
hones her beak, and listens at the basket's brink.

Sweetbriar

My palm a wing, was it,
falling in husks of darkness
on your neck, my fingers talons stinging

you to air? Is that why you writhed
as I raised you, cool mesh
that could flow into scythe

should you will? Whose
oiled rag rubbed to such luster
your scales' ungraspable pour of sesame?

Who set those flakes of ruby
in your sides, or cauterized, then sealed
the wound's euphoria

behind pliant panes? A kink of dull
red velvet, dry-tender as a pursed lip,
is garroted between two belly scales.

It tugs my inner arm,
tags me with the odor of your inner
body, which has one meaning,

which is death.
Did the falcon's crewel hook
withdraw that loop? When you fell

out the blue, a live fife rippling,
was your belly torn on the thorn
of the sweetbriar rose,

who, transpiercing, cries
I wound to heal, whose bloom
transmutes to *poetry*?

STEVE JONES

Photo courtesy of the poet

Steve, who tended a 30-acre woodlot with his lover, Ana Maria, for the last 40 years, recently moved to the 'literary' SE Corvallis. Now retired, he is the founding Co-Director of the Oregon Writing Project at Willamette University. He has 45 years of experience as an educator, instructing students in college and high school level writing, specializing in literature and creative writing. From 1980 to 2015, he worked with schools and institutions such as Oregon State University, Washington State University, Chemeketa Community College and Willamette University. As part of his vocational journey, Steve earned a bachelor's and master's degree and later completed coursework and research towards a doctoral degree at Oregon State University. Previously, he honorably served with the United States Army for several years as a paratrooper and special agent in the Intelligence Corps. Having published over 200 poems, essays and reviews, Steve maintains his status as a member of the Oregon Poetry Association and the Oregon Council of Teachers of English. His poems and poetry reviews have appeared hither and yon, including *Teachers as Writers* (Oregon Council of English, 1996), *Cloudbank, Willawaw Journal, Fireweed, Quick Fiction, Honoring Our River* (2000) and *Verseweavers*. *Bulletin of Bibliography* published his definitive bibliography of Richard Brautigan. For years, he shared friendly and astute poetry critique with Richard Dankleff and others at Dale Willey's house in Corvallis. He has also been part of the Sunnyside Writers group and was a guest editor of *Fireweed*.

Acknowledgments. Next There's Fish (Oregon Council of English, *Teachers as Writers, 1996)*; Twilight Golf *(Cloudbank)*; Traveling the Circle of Twenty Apes *(Quick Fiction)*; When People Turned to Pebbles *(Honoring Our River, 2000)*; Old Tools *(Verseweavers)*.

Next There's Fish

In my next poem I want to have fish—
puffers, eels and lying fish—among others.
I like fish.
Fish are second cousins, our briny kin,
who swim waters we only know for nine months.

My next poem will celebrate these scaly brethren
in all colors, shapes, sizes and skins.
I'd like to swim with eels,
cruise among green stalks of seaweed,
waving in warm currents or under
giant Polar caps, gliding blissfully
beneath a thousand mile ice ceiling,
basking in the cold clean water.

By the end of this poem,
I shall have quite enough swimming
for a spell—then I'll travel on great deserts—
where blowing sand will dry
all the layers of my fishy skin.

Twilight Golf

Late on a mellow July afternoon, I found
the Marysville boys milling around the first tee,
making Nassau wagers and jostling one another.
"Join us," someone called,
as I unloaded my sticks from the boot.
We teed off in flights of four, playing into the late sun,
shirtsleeves wagging in the breeze off the Marys river.
After a few holes, the course took on a dark sheen,
so the long fifth fairway startled us in the gloam,
looming up at five hundred dusky yards.
Our foursome played around to eight,
where my drive disappeared off the tee,

flying the dark pond to reappear fat and glowing
on the green, basking in the last glimpse of sun.
We lost our shadows walking in on nine
and sat on the clubhouse porch, swapping yarns
and drinking lemon beer while the last flights cruised in.

Traveling the Circle of Twenty Apes

When I was young, my dad was shot from a cannon.
We traveled with the Pickle Brothers Circus.
Dad meticulously loaded the cannon in each town—
exactly two-hundred pounds, aimed and fired
until he hit the catch-net dead center.
Mother bicycled a taut steel cable with a leather sling
in her teeth, balancing a ten-gallon aquarium of Oscars.
The circus family made a ceremony for new babies.
When I was six months old, all the mature apes
were gathered and sat in a circle.
They understood what was coming, knew the trust
shared among the strongest primates in the circus troop.
My mother tells how she unwrapped
my flannel blanket, handed me in diapers
and double-breasted T-shirt to Bruni,
the oldest mother ape. She reached out gently,
turning and nuzzling me, staring,
memorizing my features—green eyes and button nose.
All apes in attendance watched intently.
After Bruni got my looks, my smell,
she passed me to her mate, who did likewise.
So I traveled the circle of twenty apes, arm to arm.

When People Turned to Pebbles

The Kalapuya tell how the first myth age ended
when the Earth turned over—stars were born.
People became pebbles in the second,
and the third age brought a flood—
changed two-leggeds to whales, beaver and fishes.
Finally, when the world was ready,
the Kalapuya came.
Then after ten-thousand verdant years,
white-eye fur traders pushed them back
into earth, rock and valley sweet grass—
back to an earlier age.
One day, the Kalapuya will reemerge,
birthed from boulders and flowing water,
living myth that rests out of sight.

Just as the Great Spokane Flood drowned
the mountain spirits, Tcha Teemanwi
reversed the Wallama, scoured the valley,
so the Kalapuya were driven into the Earth.
Someday, these camas-gathering, story-telling people
will be reborn from the valley floor.
Till then, the Wallama soothes Kalapuya souls in fresh water.
This valley holds Kalapuya ways in trust.
The river waits.
The Kalapuya wait.
The myth rolls on.

Old Tools

Slick chisel, brace and bit, catspaw, and monkey wrench—
old tools speak to me through their dings,
rust, and scratches—the patina of hard knocks,
repairs in dark crawl-spaces, under jacked-up trucks,
and bloodied, barked knuckles.
Old tools are often the best carbon-steel, best design,
and have forgotten more tricks
than some millwrights will ever know.
Old tools in bins at Seattle Hardwick's Hardware,
yard sales and flea markets anticipate
the next rough hand, another strong grip
to bring them to bear, to repair and restore.
I wonder who will use my old tools next?

MICHAEL MALAN

Photo courtesy of the poet

Michael and Peter Sears started Cloudbank Books in 1999, publishing several poetry books until, in 2008, they started a journal. The name for the press came to them while they were eating lunch at the Valley Restaurant in Corvallis (now Evergreen Restaurant). The first issue stumbled out of the starting gate; it didn't look as though they would have enough good poetry and flash fiction to put together a quality journal. Michael held all the checks that people had sent with their submissions for several months so that he could easily refund their money if he and Peter decided not to launch the magazine. And then they got a submission from Christopher Buckley. He was always drawn to cloud imagery, he said, and liked the title of their magazine. They accepted "In Memory of the Winos at the Moreton Bay Fig Tree, Santa Barbara CA" and "New Clouds." Michael cashed the checks and *Cloudbank 1* was published a few months later. And then there was Dennis Schmitz. Long before the press, Michael had enrolled in a poetry workshop with Dennis at Cal State Sacramento (then affectionately known as "Sac State"). Shortly after the workshop was concluded, he moved to Ithaca, NY. He and Dennis corresponded a few times, then lost touch. Flash forward to 2010. While working on *Cloudbank 3*, Michael wrote to Dennis and said, "You probably don't remember me but …." Dennis had last heard from Michael when he was doing the Cornell workshops with A.R. Ammons and Robert Morgan. But he remembered Michael, knew and admired Peter's poems and thought that *Cloudbank* was a handsome magazine. Dennis submitted several poems, his "Bad Dog!" was accepted for *Cloudbank 3* and he eventually judged the first two Vern Rutsala Book Prizes (2015 and 2016). Michael is the author of *Overland Park* (poetry and flash fiction, 2017), *Tarzan's Jungle Plane* (prose poems, 2019) and *Deep Territory* (poetry, 2021), all from Blue Light Press. His work has appeared in *Epoch, Cincinnati Review, Denver Quarterly, Poetry East, Hayden's Ferry Review, Potomac Review, South Carolina Review, CutBank, Wisconsin Review, Rhino, The Christian Science Monitor, New World Writing, Washington Square Review, Tampa Review, Cincinnati Review, Chicago Quarterly* and elsewhere. Find out more about Michael at cloudbankbooks.com.

Acknowledgments. The Moving House (*Oregon Literary Review*); A New Language (*Portland Review*); A Really Good Smoke (*Wisconsin Review*); My Brother Running (*Cincinnati Review*); My Father's House (*Crosswinds*).

The Moving House

Our house moves around at night. We're sure of it. It takes a stroll around the neighborhood, then returns and settles down on its foundation. We can feel the house moving. It's sort of cool, like riding on a train, except there are no clickety-clacks. The house moves smoothly, as though it's floating on air, leisurely sailing down one street, then up another. None of our neighbors have mentioned our moving house. Mrs. Smedley hinted she may have seen it trucking past her house late one night when she couldn't sleep. "Something very large whisked past my window," she said. "And I don't believe it was a car or a truck." My wife wonders if we should tell someone about our moving house. "I don't think it's a public hazard, honey," I say to reassure her. But, to be honest, I harbor secret doubts. What if the house decides to move to Kansas or Oklahoma or some place far away? "I guess we'll cross that bridge when we come to it," I tell my wife as we settle in bed for the night. "In the meantime, *bon voyage*."

A New Language

An Oregon dictionary: beavers, ducks, big trees, snow-covered peaks, rocky coastline, umbrellas, raincoats, fishing rods, paper clips. Bricks like ships, ships like snowdrifts. The trees do not forget us. Fog moves in on little Catwoman feet. There are no centaurs in this forest, the fog says. Only paintings of Greek philosophers. And big rubber gloves. We tell the same stories over and over: the lover who fell asleep when the train rolled over, the dog that chugged back and forth between foreign cities. I met her on a Sunday.

Or maybe it was a Monday. She was planning
a trip to New Zealand. Or maybe it was India.
She was the sort of woman who could get your
attention. Already the lake behind my apartment
building was speaking a new language. As she
walked across the street, cars melted like soft cheese.

A Really Good Smoke

Smokey Robinson on the radio, singing
a sweet, lowdown tune. Governors
massing at the statehouse,
our own governor fishing for steelheads
at Lake Okabogee. I used to wear jeans
and boots like he does, back in the days
when I had a lot to prove. I was a solitary man,
a swineherd on the hogback.

Yesterday, I wrote a couple of bad poems,
then went to the poetry store to sell them.
No takers, so I went to a pawn shop
and traded the poems for a magical cigar box
with a picture of Don Juan Ortega y Gasset
on the cover. Don Juan was a minor poet
in seventeenth-century Peru,
a strong man for the junta that was

eventually snuffed out by descendants
of Chief Mazatlán, a cigar smoker
of the first magnitude. Tonight,
I am lying in a hammock looking at a bizarre
constellation in the northern sky, near
where Orion normally stands, holding his club
like a Neanderthal. A shooting star
rips through the treetops.

My Brother Running

I hear voices in the mountains.
Wildflowers speaking softly, summer
remembering winter, the moon
hiding in a forest. Someone running,
not my brother, not the moon
swimming in a frozen lake,
not the lake breathing in the sun.
I have seen a white horse in the river.
I have seen lightning in the horse's tail.

In the next valley, horses are galloping
across a shallow river, across the meadow
where winter moths are born,
the blind eyes in their wings opening.
Everything we have loved is here,
in the valley where trees are watching,
where the river carries the highway
beyond the mountains.

Coals in the campfire are like red faces,
voices in the stream like blue fire.
When night comes,
trees vanish and rivers sleep.
Each moment is a place we've been before,
a city born of its own voyage,
a village rising into being.
The openness of trees, the secrecy of mountains.
My brother running along this path, forever.

My Father's House

We knelt in a circle and howled like wolves.
What we saw was like loneliness,
like the breath of an animal
climbing a mountain in our dreams.
There is only silence in the eye of the leaf
and in the tongue of the wind.
Each moment in the forest is like a lantern
in the clouds. When I pass by
I see wolves sleeping in a pool of stone.
I am riding a river into a village of light.
Bells are ringing, the ceremony is about to begin.
A spirit moves in the chapel,
a spirit moves in the glen.
At night we see my father's house, lit from within.

JENNIFER RICHTER

Photo courtesy of the poet

Jennifer's first poetry collection, *Threshold*, won the Crab Orchard Series Open Competition (Southern Illinois University Press, 2010). *Threshold* was also an Oregon Book Award finalist and was ranked #23 on Poetry Foundation's Contemporary Bestseller List. Her second collection, *No Acute Distress,* was chosen as a Crab Orchard Series in Poetry Editor's Selection (2016) and was also an Oregon Book Award finalist. *Dear Future*, her third collection, won the Tenth Gate Prize for midcareer poets (Word Works Books, 2024). Her poems have been published in CALYX Books, *Cloudbank*, *Poetry Northwest*, *A Fierce Brightness: Twenty-five Years of Women's Poetry* (CALYX Books) and *Alive at the Center: Contemporary Poems from the Pacific Northwest* (Ooligan Press). Locally, she has been awarded an Oregon Literary Fellowship; was named "Best Poet of the Willamette Valley" in the *Corvallis Gazette-Times* Readers' Choice Awards; was chosen as one of seven Oregon poets to have work permanently installed at Kaiser Permanente Westside Medical Center in Hillsboro; was invited by Oregon State Representative Carolyn Tomei to read a poem during the opening ceremonies on the House floor; and is part of the Oregon Poetic Voices Project. Jennifer teaches undergraduate and graduate students as an Associate Professor of English and Creative Writing at Oregon State University. She has worked as an instructor of poetry in local elementary schools for the Community of Writers Program, and taught classes on poetry and text-inspired visual art for children at the Corvallis Arts Center. She has also taught poetry workshops for residents of Oak Creek Youth Correctional Facility in Albany, at the Oregon Poetry Association's Annual Conference, at the Cabin at Shotpouch Creek in the Oregon Coast Range and at Wordstock: Portland's Book Festival. The Corvallis Art Guild and Willamette Writers on the River have both invited her to lecture. She was a member of CALYX's Editorial Collective for four years and judged a number of local poetry competitions, including the Peter Sears Poetry Prize from Western Oregon University, the Lois Cranston Memorial Poetry Prize from CALYX and the Oregon Poetry Association's annual contests.

Acknowledgments. Threshold:; She Asks about Death, Then Draws; Recovery 6: The Last Word (these three poems appeared in *Threshold*); My Daughter Brings Home Bones (*No Acute Distress*); Love Poem Grounded in the Seismic Communication of Elephants (*Dear Future*).

Threshold:

where mothers prop themselves, welcoming, waving, mostly waiting. You are a frame your child passes through, the safest place to stand when the shaking starts. You brace yourself. He draws you like this, arms straight out, too stick-thin but the hands are perfect, splayed like suns, long fingers, the hands he draws for you are huge. Thresh, hold: separate the seeds, gather them back. In his pictures you all come close to holding hands, though the fingers of your family never touch; you're in the middle of all this reaching.

She Asks about Death, Then Draws

You woke knowing you'd left her. You had fallen asleep reading to her, and you woke layered in paper. She'd lain herself on your legs, making drawings, whole bodies floating. A girl's gone missing, plucked from your town close enough to the sea to sound like it: a rumbling hush of suspicion. Flash—a fish, and the pelican swooping. Your daughter knows that oceans explain what you can't: depth, distance, diagnosis that drifts you too far out. You leave her, you leave her, and then one day you'll leave her. When she asks each time you look her in the eye and lie.

Recovery 6: The Last Word

Experts like to point out things that you can't see. The woman in a vest, Whale Watching Spoken Here, hands your son binoculars, aims him at the gray. The ocean breathes like a hospital machine. You've come here many times before, alone; each time, you've left discouraged: nothing there. The experts like to say *Have faith*. You prayed for years your pain would go away; for years, you said you're fine and prayed your son believed. *Keep an eye out for the blow,* the woman says. You turn: your son is watching you. Has been watching all along, you realize. You pull him close, wrap your coat around his back. The expert checks her chart and shakes her head. *Too bad,* she says. *You just missed the best time.* She fakes a frown. You're done with these people. You drop your head and whisper to your son *No—she has no idea.* You walk together toward the car, heads down in the rain like you're about to dive. Out there, a mother whale and her son begin their long swim north today. You know it will be slow, this mother leading her new life. You'll tell him everything. *Why now?* your son will ask and you'll say *Now the mother's strong enough.*

My Daughter Brings Home Bones

and piles them on the driveway: femur, rib, jawbone with a few flat teeth attached, dozens of thin arced parts. This is for me—40 today. My birthday sent her to the woods and back. Chloe leans in on her knees, arranges the bones along a concrete seam that leads out to the street. In this next decade, she'll go: head off like today, take into her arms all she's curious about. Her line of bones makes an arrow; sun lights them like a sign. She'll go: undeniable as these bones, baffling as what animal they'd make. She's on all fours. The way I labored: some wild thing. She lays out arms and legs; the bones in line make a spine. My height. On the driveway lies my body—when it held her—inside out. The way she came: like bones. Gleaming, after living in my dark. Gleaming. So I can always find her.

Love Poem Grounded in the Seismic Communication of Elephants

So who do we know that's happily married
you ask in bed tonight after two more dear
friends split. We're quiet awhile, lie baffled
by the largest silence of our lives: no more
desk chairs rumbling upstairs; no phones
thunked to the hardwood at 2am, slipped
from our sleeping children's hands. Empty
nest, week one, I needed noise; at the fair
I bought clay elephants. Artist: age eight.
Sold only as a pair. Just like ours, I thought:
the smaller one who doesn't miss a thing,
its ears like two full sails; the other's head
tipped and listening, its trunk curled into
a question. Our son around that age said
elephants can sense what's coming. Asked
if we knew. His best friend's dad had just
moved out and left their house a wreck.
What's coming is sometimes a tsunami,
sometimes the beloved mate's vibration.
Nights now when we touch and shudder,
we let our echoes stampede every room.
This gray clay couple grown to look alike:
of course they're not the kids. Same flat
feet as ours, same wrinkly skin, all ears
except our future comes as a constant
surprise. Who knew? The elephants'
bones conduct the music when they
listen—the earth's movement trembles
in their toenails, then pulses up their
skeleton's vast map to the inner ear
which recognizes the low frequency
of natural disaster or lasting love.

Two In School
Our bodies can't let go of what they've made.
Once my daughter cut her curls and kept them
in a box. My son, three times, has asked the fairy
Please let me keep my teeth. Today my children
slip their hands from mine and and wave. At home
I smooth the tousled sheets and tuck them in.
Jennifer Richter

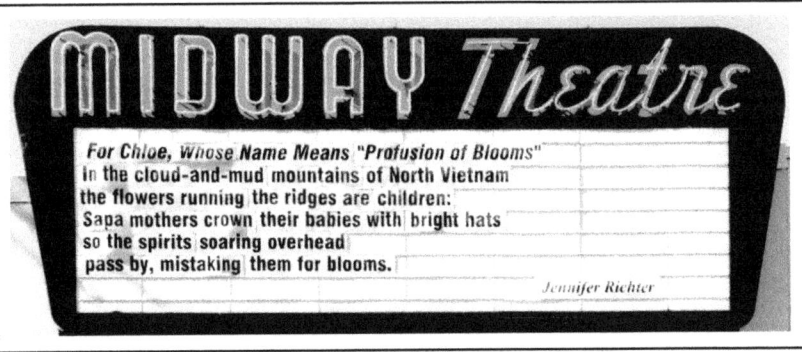

For Chloe, Whose Name Means "Profusion of Blooms"
In the cloud-and-mud mountains of North Vietnam
the flowers running the ridges are children:
Sapa mothers crown their babies with bright hats
so the spirits soaring overhead
pass by, mistaking them for blooms.
Jennifer Richter

LEX RUNCIMAN

Photo courtesy of the poet

Lex's years in Corvallis often felt like a blur, the result of too many classes to teach, too many papers to read, young children to raise and love, all the while trying to sustain some sort of reading and writing life. He sees his children, now parents, as they work hard to meet similar demands, and wonders how any of us managed. That said, these poems still reflect, one way or another, how the Willamette Valley and its proximity to the beach has always felt like home to him. Born and raised in Portland, Lex graduated from Santa Clara University (BA, 1973), worked with Madeline DeFrees and Richard Hugo at the University of Montana (MFA, 1977), and with Dave Smith at the University of Utah (PhD, 1981). He taught for 11 years at Oregon State University and 25 years at Linfield College, where he was twice named Edith Green Distinguished Professor, until his retirement. His seven books of poetry include *Luck* (Owl Creek Press, 1981); *The Admirations* (Lynx House Books, 1989), which won the Oregon Book Award; *Out of Town* (Cloudbank Books, 2004); *Starting from Anywhere* (Salmon Poetry, Ireland, 2010); *One Hour That Morning* (Salmon Poetry, 2014), which won the Julie Olds and Thomas Hellie Award for Creative Achievement; *Salt Moons: Poems 1981–2016* (Salmon Poetry, 2017); and *Unlooked For* (Salmon Poetry, 2023). His poems have received the Kenneth O. Hanson Award, the Vern Rutsala Award and the Silcox Prize. Lex has also co-edited two anthologies and co-authored three university textbooks. While living in Corvallis, he and his wife Debbie founded and ran Arrowood Books, a small press focusing on Northwest works. They now live in Portland.

Acknowledgments. One Thing; Applause; Overlook House; Beach Agates; The Waiting. (All these poems appeared in *Out of Town*.)

One Thing

In the garden
Before everything fell into its separateness,
Before everything fell apart,
The mute and noisy world sang—it was one thing—
And we had no need, no need for speech.

Pears and the mayfly hatch were one thing.
And plums withering and olives littering the floor
Were one thing. And what the spiders said spinning,
What slugs intoned, what onions in their harmonies grew,
What a kestrel's eye understood and mosquitoes knew
And what leeches and eels contemplated in their solitude
Was one thing. The arc of the sun rising and Venus rising
And the moon peering at us with its rheumy eye
And papyrus in the backwash, the kelp forest
And the swoop of bats and their dreamless sleep
And the open mouths of poppies, and sand dunes,
A drift of camas, a cane thicket, jackrabbits
And purple vetch, a stand of wheat or mustard or daisies,
A horse with its nostrils flared to the wind
Was one thing.

Afterwards, for our consolation and despair,
Our guessing and second guessing, our anger and stammer
And painful joy, we had to learn to speak to learn
How clumsy we had become
And wrong, foolish, arrogant, partial, and loud.
It's all we can do to think the world we breathe in,
The chant and rhythm of it, catching
The unsayable shape and echo
Which was one thing—speech
And silence, certainty and doubt,
The wakefulness and the sleeping,
The error and the remedy.

Applause

For preschoolers, the naturally naked, all clothing
is costume, every room a stage, simple breathing
an occasion for charming adults.
But choreographed under ceilingless lights,
music and silence surrounding them, and faced
with the formal regard of relatives and strangers,
children lack discipline: they grin and wave.
Two belong to us.

At intermission, the youngest wood nymphs return,
still costumed, garish, not quite fresh, shoeless
and easy with family who hug and praise.
Too sleepy to stay, some leave as the house lights dim
and the music assumes a new intricacy.
Some settle in to watch the height, glamor,
and toe shoes they desire.

Hours at the barre, hours before the mirror.
In leotards on rainy Tuesdays and Fridays
they have stretched, giggled, learned their own
silliness and grace—how each of us flexes, stumbles,
turns and leaps inside a body. They have learned
pliés and *relevés*, the odd spellings
of composers' and each other's names.

Friday night, 10 o'clock. The auditorium
is suffused with hair spray, perfume, and sweat.
Our programs are folded or rolled into tubes.
All the still-present company assembles.
Like something outside gravity, the curtain lifts.
And we cannot help it. Some days
it seems all we say is *no* and *no* and *no* and *no*.
Now we want to say *yes*.

Overlook House

> *See, they return, and bring us with them.*
> T.S. Eliot

Wind the ocean of air eases in lazy arcs
all S's past windows cranked open on June's last day,
Douglas firs raise up their black arms,
the drilled and the wind-seeded
tassel and berry on tall blonde stems,

and since presumably now they know,
I would like to ask two women, deceased, only memory,
where we come from, nematode and flat worm,
the deep open vents, their sulfurous ecosystems,
and to what in what dimension do we proceed?
I would like to interrogate the electrons
of this valley, neither at rest nor in motion,

the grain elevator, rolling mill, tin-
roofed barns and the hourly bells, upright poplars,
tansy and the roadside petroleum dust:
I would like to grasp simple as stone or cloud
what matter is, energy, the formula
only another more intricate naming—
I would like to hear as easily as from one daughter

in Corvallis, the other for the moment phoning
from Rome, their mother working the schedules
in Salem—I would like to hear this
because whatever it is
recurs, like the lesson day and night, blossom
and fruit, endlessly, so far—
out of reach, insistent, but quiet.

Beach Agates

Wherever they were
with kelp leaves or the worn smooth
centers of clams, or scattered
with mussels' blue neon interiors,
sea sponge and the shredded coral,

as water foamed and advanced
and gulls beat low into wind,
these waited until we found them
amber or paler yellow, quartz white
among red jasper, the blues

black in the shade. They are liquid
hardened, seamed, flawed, occluded.
They push memory such distances
imagining them humbles anyone.
Look up: all is green and silver—

the heavy surface of the sea.
But these are light, each
a particular light and smooth persistence—
they ought to testify.
They ought to say something

beyond random currents, tidal order.
They are the origin and dream of glass.
Whatever they say is impersonal:
whatever it is is beautiful.

The Waiting

Late bees convene, they interrogate the porch.
Paper wasps held together by god knows what
visit the seat-sprung, the cane back chairs.
Dark snow goes uphill in narrower runnels
on mountains hazed into distance.
Tired summer hangs on.

We are not met.
The hand we seek, the one in dreams
that laves our faces and hums the unremembered song—
the hand, the gesture and all its benevolence
darkens nothing, offers nothing.

If we knew for certain what was needed.
If we knew precisely the process, step-by-step,
rules for the dance, orders for the colors
of one bougainvillea, lilac, or Norway maple.
If we knew why they sing in our eyes.
If we could say the name, the perfect sounds
for ground we love. That, and the common litany—
how this becomes this becomes mango
and bird of paradise, cocoa bean, skunk cabbage.
If we could say why.
If we could know the title of any rainwater, river, well
water, the miles and endless minutes
in the clear glass we drink from. If
we could rouse and tease the dead
or ourselves unborn.
But we are not met.

The harrowed fields are so carefully groomed
they've become sculpture, all parallels and contours.
Blackberries flatten. The long shadows of 6:20 pm
stretch out and recline under an unstarred blue.
The light goes rose, golden. We talk.

PETER SEARS

Photo courtesy of Anita Helle and the Estate of Peter Sears

Peter, poet and teacher, served as Oregon's seventh Poet Laureate from 2014 to 2016, and was active in the state's literary community for more than 40 years. Over those years, he published collections of poetry as well as books on teaching writing. *Small Talk*, published by Lynx House Press in 2014, gathered poems from his eight previous collections and added 30 new poems; *Long Day* followed posthumously in 2019. He died in 2017. Peter came to Oregon in 1974 to serve as writer-in-residence at Reed College and went on to become one of the state's most celebrated poets, educators and literary activists. A graduate of Yale and the Iowa Writers Workshop, Peter taught writing at many universities and colleges besides Reed, including Bard College, Portland State University, PCC, the Pacific University MFA Low-Residency Program and through Mountain Writers and Fishtrap. He served as Dean of Students at Bard College (1980–1983), was community services coordinator for the Oregon Arts Commission (1985–1998) and director of the Oregon Literary Coalition. His work has appeared in national publications such as *Saturday Review, The New York Times, The Atlantic, Mother Jones, The Christian Science Monitor* and *Rolling Stone*, as well as in literary magazines such as *Field, New Letters, Iowa Review, Poetry Northwest, Antioch Review, Ploughshares* and *Seneca Review*. His poetry collections include *Tour: New and Selected Poems, The Brink* and *Green Diver*; his books on teaching writing include *Secret Writing* and *I'm Gonna Bake Me a Rainbow Poem*. *The Brink* was named one of Oregon's 150 best books by the Oregon State Library in 2009. Other achievements include an Award for Contribution to Oregon Writing, Willamette Writers, 2008; Western States Book Award for Poetry, Western States Arts Federation, 2000 (for *The Brink*); Stewart A. Holbrook Award for Contribution to Oregon Literary Life, Literary Arts, Inc., 1999; Award of Honor and Appreciation, Oregon State Library, 1988; and a Poetry Fellowship from the Oregon Arts Commission. Peter also co-founded (with Michael Malan) Cloudbank Books in Corvallis in 2001; co-founded (with Kim Stafford) Friends of William Stafford in 1997, serving as director in 1998; founded Oregon Literary Coalition in 1993, a coalition of writers and non-profit organizations for networking and advocacy, serving as director through 2009; and initiated Across the River, the first multi-state literary project in the US, funded by the NEA, OAC and WSAC. Locally, he managed Rubberstampmadness, Inc. Peter is survived by his wife, Anita Helle, and his daughter, Rivers Elizabeth Sears.

Acknowledgments. Snow at Night (*Orion*); Traffic Jam on the Ross Island Bridge (*Zyzzyva*); American Hero: A Poem Made into a Movie (*Beloit Poetry Journal*); Bummer (*Long Day*, Lynx House Press, posthumously, copyright Peter Sears 2019); Who's the Who Walking Beside Me? (*Long Day*, Lynx House Press, posthumously, copyright Peter Sears 2019). (All these poems were selected by Anita Helle and Michael Malan.)

Snow at Night

I am so far away
that from there I can hear myself talking to someone
and an echo like when you turn away from a river
and you can't tell
if it's the river right then
or a sound of the river echoing through you.

I want to go there and watch in the eddies near the shore.
The caught sticks turning, then popping back,
then turning again,
as if they would break in two to shake free.

I'm like the snow at night in the field.
Most of the time you can't see it, then it glistens.

Traffic Jam on the Ross Island Bridge

I am knuckled in here on the Ross Island Bridge,
heading west, toward the West Hills of Portland.
The hills are ridged by trees in silhouette
against the sunset. Strands of clouds loll over the trees,
sink into them, and snag. One strand settles in the trees
like a big, gray nest. If there is no Northwest bird
that lays its eggs in such a nest, inventing it is my job.
My potter friend and I will envision the bird.
I will tell my friend that white sunset
comes down on the nest and shimmers it;
and darkness, thick with rain, pushes the light
down into the trees. There is not enough sky for rain
to get down easily. The rain is slowed by rain
below it. Why hurry? This is Oregon, rain is lazy here.
Wind shoots rain up in sheets that topple back
and fall through themselves. Between the tree line and
the darkness falling are planes of light,
measuring miles across. Rain does not faze them.

These slabs slide through themselves,
across the entire city. I'd love to have one hover
over my backyard some early evening,
and take friends out to toast it.

American Hero: A Poem Made into a Movie

      for Dennis Meiners

Silhouetted on a ledge, the grand beast known
in local legend as the Vanilla Gorilla! My posse
tumbles like dominoes. I take my fiberglass bow,
lay an arrow in, and vissst!—my arrow snips
him off, punctures his little ear so bulbous red
it looks inside out. He goes dummy on the ledge,
tips over. People want hair, clumps of it, parades,
a national holiday. Cubs, Brownies, Legionnaires,
and Miss American Aphrodite sipping warm milk
with nuns and the DAR, and girls with skin
like bubble gum, dancing the squid, the tongue,
the pneumatic drill. I'm led to a reviewing stand
where a retired WAC called Sizzles proclaims me
"Hero!" and a bear of a jukebox rolls to my chest
swelling. My heartbeat is recorded for the country.

I run for the woods, hug a tree. Something gives.
I want to be a crowd. My feet feel like galoshes.
There's Miss American Aphrodite! She's the girl
next door, girl with parents, girl with other guy.
She stares at her drink. Her ice is melting.
I feel as big as a ranch. She's coming up,
I hear her bubbling. Her face is a swimming pool.
I want to be a helicopter, hover over her, dangle
my arms to her. We go for a spin, run every light
and go the wrong way up a one-way. Faster.

Bummer

The turkey with the bum leg takes forever
to cross into my neighbor's backyard. I'm afraid
he is going to die in my yard. His buddies prance by,
flicking their heads from side to side,
as if they are lost kings looking for a Ferrari dealership.
They bump him, which means get out of my way.
The world bumps me too,
but I don't have a leg to drag along
or buddies who bump me. Bummer—that's what I call him—
could use a little buddy who thinks he's the greatest.
Bummer doesn't have much time and with that bum leg,
he can't get up into the Doug firs to sleep
like the other turkeys. He sleeps at the base
of the big pine in my neighbor's back yard.
I've seen him poke out that head
From under the long branches that sweep the ground
And shake it and shake it.

Who's the Who Walking Beside Me?

I get up the nerve to ask people—
Relax, that's just the way we are,
always feeling there is a second one of us.

Sure, but what help is that?
I just go on rolling pebbles
over and over in my mouth,

not too loud, no. They thrash around
in my head like eels when my brother
and I lifted the pot off the bottom of the pond,

into the boat, and opened the lid.
We threw the pot back in so hard
we almost fell overboard.

But that was my brother,
not the one walking beside me,
the one who feels, most of the time,

like me clearing my throat.
If only I could reach down
and yank it out.

MATTHEW SHENODA

Photo courtesy of the poet

Born in California, Matthew is a Coptic American poet and writer whose parents emigrated from Egypt. He received a BA from Oregon State University in 1999 and an MFA from the University of Arizona in 2001. Exploring diasporic identity and pan-Africanism, Matthew is the author of the following poetry collections: *The Way of the Earth* (TriQuarterly Books, 2022); *Tahrir Suite: Poems* (TriQuarterly Books, 2014), winner of an Arab American Book Award; *Seasons of Lotus, Seasons of Bone* (BOA Editions, 2009); and *Somewhere Else* (Coffee House Press, 2005), which received an American Book Award from the Before Columbus Foundation, the inaugural Hala Maksoud Award for Emerging Voice and was named one of the year's top debut books by *Poets & Writers Magazine*. With Kwame Dawes, he co-edited *Bearden's Odyssey: Poets Respond to the Art of Romare Bearden* (TriQuarterly Books, 2017). He was also the editor of Kwame Dawes's *Duppy Conqueror: New & Selected Poems* (2013). Matthew's poetry, reviews and essays have appeared in publications such as *Columbia Poetry Review, Indiana Review, Oregon Literary Review, Prairie Schooner, Publishers Weekly, Sou'wester Magazine, To Topio: Poetry International, Vassar Review, Washington Square Review, World Literature Today* and *The Yale Review*. Additionally, his writing has appeared in numerous anthologies and he has received a Lannan Literary Residency as well as grants from the California Arts Council and the Ford Foundation. Matthew began his teaching career in the College of Ethnic Studies at San Francisco State University, where he taught for nearly a decade. He has since held several faculty and administrative positions at various institutions, including: assistant provost and faculty member in the School of Critical Studies at the California Institute of the Arts; associate provost for social equity and inclusion and professor at Rhode Island School of Design. Presently, he is professor and chair of the Department of Literary Arts and affiliated faculty in Africana Studies and the Brown Arts Institute at Brown University. Matthew is a founding editor of the African Poetry Book Fund and both the African Book Series and the On African Poetry book series (University of Nebraska Press).

Acknowledgments. Somewhere Else; Where We Come from; Reclaiming the Classroom (after *Three for Phil McGee*); Al-Mansūra (Nile Blues); Dispatches from the New World. (All these poems appeared in *Somewhere Else*.)

Somewhere Else

It is here on this ridge
exposed to the orange dusk
of mountain autumn
that the story begins.

Buck wood for the stove
feel the heat of shoulder to tendon
greet the mule deer
and water the garden again.

In rhythm, with song
when the ax begins to blend with wind
carry on to warmer days
on the river's open banks
where the fervor of healing is found in water.
Flow from one origin to another—
there is never a place where we cannot begin
where the current is ancient, the wind is young
teaching each other like the ax and the wood.

Carve a place for dignity
plant a seed and pray for rain
for sun
for understanding outside your self.

There will come a day when they say:
who do you think you are
and another day will come
for you to tell.

On that day the story will appear
but do not tell of yourself

tell the story of the staff that blossomed in the desert
or the one about your enemy's greatest victory

tell the story of somewhere else

Where We Come From

semi-automatic machine fire
barreling through
freedom for hire

our homelands becoming
first world garbage dumps

too much internal posturing
not enough external interrogation

rising from cane fields & potted mint leaves
na'nā' breath & cellophane feet

eating *rummān* & *tamr hind*
escaping into juice-glitter

       in places where the list of murdered
       surpasses the dead by natural causes

hunger is not the birthright of the children

retinas glare with coals of sandstone

muddied waters are the fertile of servile

       in places where the list of murdered
       surpasses the dead by natural causes

children dream of parrot fish in coral sunshine

dusty streets are filled with bright fabric
'cause weaving is the art of prayer

trash heaps rise like sky-water

doves fly over waves crying

in places where the list of murdered
    surpasses the dead by natural causes

mirrors reflect lies

'afarīt lurk in crop soil

children learn from coal-burned corn

hieroglyphs speak truths

conquest sleeps in the neighbor's house

people hide colonial shoes under beds

someone walks on the dunes of ruin

we sing reality
through blue lotus songs

    in places where the list of murdered
    surpasses the dead by natural causes

politicians pay surgeons
to sew their eyes shut
& launch cannons in their ears

---

na'nā': Arabic; mint
rummān: Arabic; pomegranate
tamr hind: Arabic; tamarind
'afarīt: Arabic; evil spirits or ghosts, similar to the West Indian "Duppy"

Reclaiming the Classroom (after *Three for Phil McGee*)

> for John-Carlos Perea, colleague and composer of the struggle, brother on bass

The drummer warms his song
by splitting a blade of grass.
Somewhere between dewdrops
and wet earth, the rhythm begins.

      Sing sweet friend, sing
Pay tribute in times of tore-up nations
on days when the sun spells
g i v e   t h a n k s
and clouds remind us of those we've tried to forget.

John-Carlos you tell time in fret increments

bouncing into notions of remembrance
your bass songs, woven with liquid and flesh
like pomegranates split with broken glass
the "urban" Indian moving through city blocks
pulling mottoes from the sky
making music-memory

John-Carlos you wrote this one for our elders
educators of pavement wisdom, asphalt blues

wrote with verve
rote with verve

reclamation songs fluttering from
saxophone licks called back on a trip gone north

this is how it feels to remember
to remember the horizon before sunset
to understand that once we've gone, we've just begun
this journey, this first-dance, the dance
we bring to our classrooms
the dance you keep tucked at your nape
as an offering

and with your songs
your offerings
you gave me San Francisco
shaped it into something tangible
made the bridges my Nile
so I could give thanks again
and understand that brothers live near every river
and brothers sing in every voice
that in a time of rampant bombings
an offered song can bring us peace
or move us to something greater
that thing that's greater than peace
that prayer we call justice

to teach us to release
and catch ourselves again
syncopated pomegranates
flecked with marrow red

rejuvenation
rejoice
rejuvenation
we're taking this one back
we're gonna take this one back, way back,

back to the day when
yeah when yeah
when we could when we
could can can
like the colors of the toucan
we can dance

this first dance

just as dance

just as dance

justice dance

Al-Manṣūra (Nile Blues)

    for my pops

In villages where wealth is food
my sisters cook for peace
and I lie sweating, wondering
where do I go from here?

In the city where my father was born
the Nile Delta
where blues squeaked out
of *ʿūd* string treble
banks riffing to the dance
of smooth-flowing water

My father takes me back
to that place
where pains made way to a resister
to you
who made this man a man
in a time of warring nations

I take these words
from beneath the wings you gave me
and make them brave
to combat all our histories

Al-Manṣūra: Arabic; a city in the Nile Delta
ʿūd : Arabic; a traditional short-necked Egyptian lute

Dispatches from the New World Order

Standing on solid earth
It is clear that we have lost something
In this space of forever crossings and collapsible borders
This space of translucent snaking and palm shadow adaptations

We used to have jobs, he says,
something to help sustain us,
something to reaffirm our humanity
through the ancient wisdom of work
now we have nothing but dissipating time
a horizon that reeks of death
we learn the steps for a coming bone dance
we are destined to be skeletons encircling ravines

How do you articulate
indigenous sense that rises from streets like mist?
How do you convey
the reality that land can teach culture's song?

We eclipse the moon with styrofoam
and ravage ourselves with jingle madness
articulating a corporate narrative
and suffocating the breath of story-speakers

we crawl through the epithet forests
craving the singular answer
forgetting that our fallen brothers are the only soothsayers on this land
and their voices are anything but lonesome

The Willamette Literary Guild
and the Corvallis Public Library
present

Poets of Faith

an interfaith reading faeaturing poetry by
A.Y. Lafi
Steve Jones
Steven Sher
Roger Weaver
Jason Younker
Chris Anderson
Donna Henderson
Eric Wayne Dickey
Charmaine Black-Olive
Linda Williamson Gelbrich

connection
& healing through
poetry & song

2:00 - 4:00 pm
October 21, 2001
main meeting room
Corvallis Public Library

refreshments

LITERARY Cabaret

Winter/Spring Cabaret

Readings by Local Literary Artists

*Corvallis Arts Center
Friday, March 13, 1992
7:30 P.M.*

Sponsored by the Willamette Literary Guild and the Corvallis Arts Center

Light refreshments offered free but donations gladly accepted

STEVEN SHER

Photo by Bill Apple

New York-born, Steven lived in Corvallis (until 2003) for almost 20 years. He now lives in Jerusalem. His writing (poetry, short fiction, folktales, essays, satire and features) has appeared worldwide since the 1970s. His 20 books include three recent poetry collections: *When They Forget* (New Feral Press, 2022), *What Comes from the Heart: Poems in the Jewish Tradition* (Cyberwit, India, 2020) and *Contestable Truths, Incontestable Lies* (Dos Madres Press, 2019). A sampling of his publications includes *Ascent, Confrontation, European Judaism, The Georgia Review, The Greenfield Review, Hubbub, Kansas Quarterly, The Louisville Review, The MacGuffin, The Midwest Quarterly, The Nebraska Review, Poet Lore, Prairie Schooner, Rain City Review, Santa Barbara Review, Solo, Spillway, Talking River Review, Tar River Poetry, Tiferet, Valparaiso Poetry Review* and *Witness*. His anthology appearances include *Blood to Remember: American Poets on the Holocaust; Veils, Halos & Shackles: International Poetry on the Oppression and Empowerment of Women; With Signs & Wonders: An International Anthology of Jewish Fabulist Fiction; Proposing on the Brooklyn Bridge: Poems about Marriage; Amethyst and Agate: Poems of Lake Superior; The Second Genesis: an Anthology of Contemporary World Poetry;* and *New Voices: Contemporary Writers Confronting The Holocaust*. Steven's work has been featured by Symphony Space (Selected Shorts) and Poetry In Motion, and was an Oregon Book Award finalist (for *Traveler's Advisory*, 1994) and a Pushcart Prize nominee. In 2018, he received the Glenna Luschei Distinguished Poet Award. Since 1977, he has taught at Oregon State University, University of Oregon, Willamette University, Western Oregon University, LBCC, University of North Carolina-Wilmington, Spalding University (director, creative writing), Yeshiva University, Brooklyn College and Manhattan College. Writing workshops/residencies include Literary Arts, Inc., Poets House, Coos Head Writers Workshop, Tumble Words, The Rural Readers Project/Story Line Press, Oregon State Poetry Association, NEA's Creativity & Aging Initiative and NY Public Library's Poetry in the Branches. He has headlined the Catskill Poetry Festival, Outloud Festival and San Luis Obispo Poetry Festival. A graduate of City College of New York and University of Iowa's School of Journalism, he received his MFA from Brooklyn College where he worked with John Ashbery. For 50+ years, Steven has served as an editor and writing consultant. While living in Corvallis, he presided over the Willamette Literary Guild (1992–2001), developing programs such as Poets of Faith; 100 Years, 100 Writers: Celebrating Past and Present Corvallis-Benton County Writing; and the Diverse Voices writing series. He also served on the Oregon State University Press editorial board (1981–1986). Find out more about Steven at steven-sher-poetry.wixsite.com/writing.

Acknowledgments. The Skipping Stone (Finishing Line Press); Secrets *(Mudfish)*; The Man Who Brought His Own Food *(Prairie Schooner)*; The House of Washing Hands *(Hubbub)*; Revealing What Is Hidden *(Jewish Currents)*.

The Skipping Stone

    for Nancy

From the mud of the green-scum pond,
she drew a flat round rock, a smooth and perfect
fit inside her palm. She rubbed and flipped it
one hand to the other, let it slip between
her fingers like a charm. Soon she knew
the black stone like a child knows a parent's hand.
She took it with her everywhere. The years passed.
Once when her bag spilled open on the bed,
her new husband saw the stone and picked it up.
Making imaginary sidearm throws, he claimed
that he could skip her round flat beauty
twenty times before it sank. She told him
he'd be throwing love away and rubbed
the stone until the smell of small green apples
and the summer sun on the still pond returned,
then placed it back inside her bag.
Soon babies came. She stuffed the bag
with gloves and gum, with empty wrappers,
scraps of paper, books and boots, a tub
of wipes and toys. They dumped it all onto the rug.
The curious smoothness of her stone
excited their small hands. When they left home,
once on their own, she feared they took
the best of her away. Discovering the bag
she hadn't used in years, she dumped its contents
on the kitchen table. The flat black stone
now tumbled out, again a perfect fit inside her hand.
She rubbed it as she had when she was young.
A sudden breeze swept through the trees,
brushing her cheek. She caught the scent
of small green apples, sensed the stillness
of the pond, her parents' presence,
placed the stone beside old photographs
and gifts spread on her dresser. Her life
appeared as one flat stretch of water,
the past retrieved one bounce at a time,

where nothing, while the stone
skipped over, ever sank.

Secrets

The secret of the wind, papa's hot
breath, blows in her bones.

The reason for the rain, her stormy
temperament, goes beyond clouds.

Our daughter's twitching sleep will
take her one hundred and eighty

degrees around the sheet
and so she'll learn this room

before she walks, hear her fate
among the shadows talk

before she feels it kiss
her fat milk cheeks.

The Man Who Brought His Own Food

    for Natalee Moinester

She doesn't remember his name
or anything he might have said—
she was too young—but only
that the man brought his own food,
a grocery bag set on the countertop
beside the phone, some fresh things
wrapped in plastic in the fridge,

and he wouldn't eat from their plates.
With some prompting, she will say
he was an old friend of her father's
she had met for the first time
who wore a yarmulke and in the morning
seemed to move his lips but out came
silence as he stood and shook
wrapped in black straps and a white shawl
before his book off by himself
while she watched cartoons, yet
he didn't seem to notice the spectacular
view of the mountains behind the house,
his eyes half-closed, his shape gone limp.
Maybe then the girl first guessed
her father was this way before,
so too the grandfather she never knew
among those strange and chanting
men at once familiar in her dreams.

The House of Washing Hands

The sound of running water
fills our house, an ocean's
timeless rise and fall.
My son's discovered soap
and water calm the soul
and heal the flesh, as blood
will purify the heart.
All his childhood he has
instructed guests to scrub.
Sometimes he will wash his hands
till they begin to peel. For weeks
the pink new skin will probe
his palms, reside in cracks.
And he will be oblivious,
albeit blessed, to his obsession,
as I am of mine: twisting

faucets off so tightly
none can turn them on.
A son and father drawn
to water's excess, discovering
love exists within extremes.

Revealing What Is Hidden

    for Amy Buccola

Here live Jews who know the work
we've yet to do: a lumberjack
whose saplings reclaim clear-cut hills;
the garlic growers who have saved
red clay beneath their nails;
an herbalist who will enlist
the mysteries of tinctures;
the odd-job Jew who harvests
seaweed, rose hips, chanterelles;
the weaver, painter, poet, dancer—
revealing grace within all things;
the massage practitioner and macrobiotic
chef, those who listen to the needs
of flesh; the nurse, who never
turns from pain, beside the bed.
I tell you this to dispel the myth
that we're all rich, that we're unhappy.

LINDA VARSELL SMITH

Photo by Court Smith

Linda is a retired creative writing teacher of workshops and at the local community college. Her literary publications class at LBCC produced the award-winning *The Eloquent Umbrella* to showcase writing and art of the community. She was an editor at CALYX Books for over 30 years and served as president of the Oregon Poetry Association. She received the 2020 Pat Banta Award for promoting poets and poetry. Currently president of PEN Women of Portland, Linda is also a member of several writing groups and belongs to Writing the Wrongs to Rights huddle formed from the Women's March. She is an avid cooperative and competitive Scrabble player, enjoys poetry readings, arts and crafts fairs and art shows, and studies astrophysics and diverse spirituality. She lives among over 3000 angels, Swedish folk art, elves and fairies, and seasonal miniatures in her mini-museum with husband Court. Linda has lived in Corvallis for over 50 years, writing 27 poetry books and 12 novels. She has published 26 books of poetry.

Acknowledgments. Demidonne in an Antique Shop (*Black Stars on a White Sky*); The Sand Spider (*Black Stars on a White Sky*); Hallowing Ground (*Black Stars on a White Sky*); The Land Octopus (*Poet Lore*); Shifting Attention (*Beyond Windows*).

Demidonne in an Antique Shop

    Lincoln City, Oregon

Demidonne ... metronome man ...
Miniature ... metal ... mechanical man
clicks his seven motions
for 1919 advertising.

A mute stringless puppet,
he perches behind eleven calligraphed pages
which flip mechanically for customers to skim and scan.
Some torn reveal metal spines between sheets.
Some pageless disclose an iron fist of page support.
Left hand holds a wand; points to magical promises.
His right glides glibly with each ad.
His eye brows windshield-wipe his forehead;
ping-pong eyes roll back and forth like a spectator's.
Pinocchio nose long with lies.
Rusty dimple on his chin.
Lips red as a recent scratch.
Hatless, bushy black hair
falls to dust-speckled black patched suit.
Shirt color-rings in turtleneck.
This clownish business man now sells himself.

As he flops his obsolete wares
a small note card offers him for $2000.
A full page newspaper ad can be $1500
and next day stoke a fire to flame.
He has been overhauled by a master mechanic;
for sound you can add a tape in the background.

He is a pre-audio-animatronic species
unlike those that populate the land of Disney
as mechanotherapy for nostalgia.
Lacking three-dimensional space age animation
the demidonne, an acned adolescent,
repeats his seven motions

a hustling homunculus
amidst dusty discards
a graven image of greed.

The Sand Spider

      South Beach, Oregon: December

Sound blurs with the surf under winter sun.
Football squeals, motorcycle peals;
a saw gnaws driftwood to the core.
I lie here
with weathered wood
waiting for warmth and zest.
Silently a red spider
crawls on my fanned hand.
I flick the nail-sized nuisance
to flounder in the sand, yet
the spider rolls and rights itself.
With fingers crooked like spider legs,
I poke; then meander and mound
webs in squeaky sand.
Stunned, the spider surveys
unnecessary ridges,
domed mountains and smooth holes.
With octopus legs it swims in sand avalanches.
A Lem on a pocked planet, it moves toward mountains.

The angle was too steep; the spider fell on its back.
Legs roil air. I lift and launch it
as a spiderling ballooning in spring.
Landing, the spider hauls toward driftwood.
The spider, a sun burnt spot, is bright on the beach.
I am cold and dull as a beached stone out of water.

Hallowing Ground

    for Kip (1992)

We climbed a fog-bound hill;
carried our beloved son's ashes
to be buried by relentless rain.
Fog tamped ashes into moistened ground
until one day ashes were gone.
We yearned for the warmth of sun.

Daily tears resurrect him. Sun
lifts the dew on the dampened hill.
Leaves shroud. Seeds cradle. Seasons gone.
An alder breeds from the ashes,
burrows roots in hardened ground
massaged by softening rain.

Can pain fall gently as rain
or joy lighten days as sun?
We tread hallowed ground.
Our recovery remains uphill.
Our hands cannot feel ashes
or caress flesh forever gone.

When laughter blooms, some numbness goes.
When grief tugs, memories rein.
Our lives, like fog blurred by ashes,
tendril toward renewing sun;
seek haven on his lofty hill
and hope not found on common ground.

Sow particles of life when death has ground
hearts to fragments, wholeness gone.
We clamber the clearing hill
across stones speckled with motes of rain.
We see dust in rays of sun
and remember hand-thrown ashes.

With warmth drawn from cooled ashes
we step for more solid ground.
Mist clears. We know our son
is with us always. Love's never gone.
Our grandson Haidan Regn's
placenta nourishes life on that hill.

On a tended hill we left ashes
tendered by rain on greyed ground.
Heavy grief gone, lightened by sun.

The Land Octopus

The land variety of octopus
is of ten glossy white as wet stones
with color fins on its sides.
Its blimpish body is headless.
Nerves wired in inner skin
conduct at a flip of a switch.
Its brain remains undetected.

Eyeless, vestigial transparent lids
are often curtained from sun and moon.
When led, there is no need to see.

Sucker bearing arms of the sea species
are specialized on land.
Sewage, water, electric lines;
leveling jacks, hitch, tires
tentacle to the ground and poles.
These tentacles do not coil to crunch,
but twirl rubbery tendrils
or shaft solidly straight.
They draw and discharge
to service others;
sporadically connect then
retract within.

Unlike the soft sea species,
it has metalized shell—
more like a crustacean.
Its awnings breathe air like gills.
Breezes wave over *too* low grass;
Black top lies *too* flat to touch its body.
Rain stripes road dirt;
rusts until the bulk is crushed away.

Its enlarged shape is
to hold its prey.
The door mouths people in.
They churn inside its belly.
Tourists swallowed from the world
peer out its apertures.
Land octopi cannot digest their prey.
They remain hollow.

Wantonly violated, they become
impregnated people
who gestate in their metal womb
until birthed through its rigid opening.
Land octopi remain sterile.

Bulbous genitals hang near the hitch.
They mate with cars.
Hooked by cars for movement
they migrate asphalt and concrete
searching for landings.
Cars command when to blink light.
Cars uncouple and roll away.

Land octopi park neverland.
Never root. Never firm a foundation.
Nestless, restless,
the earth flattens for them.

Shifting Attention

A bluetiful jay hops down the rock wall steps,
pecks the lawn, leisurely strolls near
backyard wall and flies to rhododendron.

During my watch five butterflies cruise
the garden. Two dance side by side,
circle each other, before higher flights.

The back-warming sun casts dark shadows.
Tuffs of gray and white seed puffs fluff
around me, I blow them away.

Only three dandelions left. Bees keep away.
In Washington murder hornets decapitate
bees and feed them to their larva. Here?

Bugs whiz by. A fly lands on my thumb.
Unseen bird chirps, wind chimes clang
until droned out by two power mowers.

Both start and stop repeatedly. The eastside
mower angrily shouts to himself and yells at a
red azalea. Luckily there's a fence between us.

Someone to the west whistles for a dog
probably fifteen times for two barks. Four
beeps from a car and I'm done.

A stellar jay swoops in front of me in a cross
lawn flight. A sparrow perches on the back fence.
I am torn between warm beauty and retreat.

SUSAN SPADY

Photo courtesy of Beth Littlehales and Emily Spady

Susan was born in Eugene and grew up in Bandon, OR. She graduated from Lewis & Clark College in 1969, then left Oregon to live for two years in Chicago and seven in Alaska. She was then variously rooted in Western Oregon, earning an MFA in Creative Writing at the University of Oregon in 1986. In 1992, Susan moved to the Corvallis area, and in 1993, she was chosen as Oregon's first William Stafford Poet. Susan published poems in *Poetry Northwest, CALYX Journal, Northwest Review, Calapooya Collage* and two anthologies, *From Here We Speak: An Anthology of Oregon Poetry* and *Millennial Spring*. An avid organic gardener, she was also an incredible cook and inventive seamstress. She was a wonderful mother to three children, Greg, Beth and Emily. Susan suffered from bipolar disorder in her later years and died by suicide in 1999.

Acknowledgments. Carrying Eggs (*Poetry Northwest*); Rock Paper Scissors (*Poetry Northwest*); Pot-Pot-Pots (*CALYX Journal*); Underpants (*CALYX Journal*); Pretending (*Millennial Spring*).

Carrying Eggs

If you're sure you won't spill them,
Grandma said, and I held my breath
from the hen house to her kitchen,
afraid the still-warm eggs would hatch
in mid-air. They were the-world-
on-my-shoulders my father always told me
I couldn't carry. Shaky, I set them down.

Years later, I walked past protesters wearing
black arm bands, and hugged
books to my chest. My arms ached
with their weighty signs. When I raised my hand
in class I could hardly speak.

Now I have this girl-
child with her swagger and trumpet
voice. She's barely a year
as a hundred thousand eggs form
in her miniature baskets.
She will march, shout, make waves,
and they won't spill. She is their reckless
keeper, and they, spirals of song
drifting the fragile
earth's breath.

Rock Paper Scissors

He opens out the game board—
a parking lot again—
pulls into the farthest space.
Hunkers behind the wheel,
sends the children lugging their bags
over icy pavement. It's Sunday,
they've been to Daddy's church,

come home pale as snow
to stacked beds. Nightmares
smack their walls like frantic birds.
My son takes sewing scissors,
cuts my clothes, cringes in the closet.
At Goodwill I hunt for new ones
as they whirl the racks. I've lost

the fifty dollar bill, three days
needing groceries. My daughter screams
while I pry her piggy open. It's folded
like her tiny secret love notes.

Bundled up, we walk to feed the ducks,
whose water closes now
to sheeted ice. We carry home the stale
bread. They tell me how he changes
rules to win: as rock,
he grinds paper; forbids them, in his house,
to say my name.

       They bite,
swing toy trucks. *Here hit these—*
I throw pillows, punch until
I'm weak. They're playing in the bath,
rock, paper, scissors, Mommy,
which are you? I answer.
Water.

Pot-Pot-Pots

Steel, stainless, smooth as
silk my hands can't help
but stroke, fat shapes of knobs and
handles, curvy lids, weight of triple-clad
copper bottoms that won't scorch butternut
soup or Roma tomatoes simmering. Music
of lid to rim, rings of sound singing
the soup's steaming octaves; sheer dizzying
walls of light that whisper
fall, fall into
pot-pot-pots.

    Ah, yes! How I've longed
for every man I've loved to buy for me these
last-a-lifetime, gleaming, utilitarian
tools of my trade—to pull out his wallet and say,
"Of course, my Sweet, of course you deserve
the *very* best pot-pot-pots"—for those
stirrings, those savory, rich aromas,
and scourings—

    and so now, when I've bolted, jobless,
from my marriage, my house, my garden, and my warped,
dented, cheap-to-begin-with-twenty-year-old
pots and pans—now, when all my money cowers in the bank
for next month's rent—why would I, now, leave the store

coveting? I go get money,
give it all to the expensive kitchen shop,
carry the box to my shabby rented room
and open it like a wedding present, the white
tissue rustling, the pans
emerging in rings of light—

    for how many men—
having made their stew—offered me
vessel outside my body to fill with my own

elixir? To hold my fragrant pudding, my
pungent soup, my hot smooth fruity sauce? Oh,
my pot-pot-pots, your drumness; oh, your fine
drumness! I open and taste
the vows stirring, and marry my-
self.

Underpants

            showed when girls climbed the monkey
bars so some girls didn't. Some who did
would kick a boy in the mouth if he got smart.
Others showed off their pink and lace,

wiggled high overhead as boys yelled
London, France. Earthbound, I sucked in
my pot belly and tried to stand in some regal way
so a book on my head, when I walked,

wouldn't fall Daddy said. Mine
were never panties, were plain
as oxfords correcting my feet. By junior high

those fancy pants climbers were cheerleaders
flirting from under their minis, tossing
smiles at the crowd through pearled lips.
They did splits: hello,

from between our legs! And my book
slid off frontways now, sweaters revealing
empty puckers, bras I made only a dent in
and slouched to hide. I didn't think much

about underpants. I was sealed shut,
spoke sarcastic nothings to boys, prayed
every night for God to make me
sinless and new. While pompoms exploded

like fireworks from cheerleaders' fingers, I sat
in the bleachers distorting my face
on my saxophone, wearing the Pep Band's sickly
gold, my disdain for those highkickers

but it's all right. Because first
I stopped going to Sunday School
and then wearing underpants
opened my stride
to winds that long full skirts

gathered in. I visited London and France,
climbed stairways with risers of blue sky
over men always looking
but never upward.

Pretending

> *Let's pretend this is the toothbrush
> that the egg carton loves so much.*
> Emily (age 2)

And so it is in that other world—
things love each other, even
things that are standing in
for other things, for every-
thing stands in for love, for some-
thing beyond itself which shines
through it. And so we must ask
what it is we stand for, what shines
for us, through us, and if no-
thing, then why, and what
have we forgotten; ask how
we could forget the light in every
cell and atom, forget this world,
this dance of light and love—
forget that by pre-
tending, we make it so?

River Songs
FROM THE WILLAMETTE RIVER DIPTYCH

An Anthology of River Poems

Riven 1

Poetry Journal

MICHAEL SPRING

Photo by Sara Backer

During the time Michael lived in Corvallis (1993–2003), he worked as an assistant manager and a used book buyer for The Corvallis Book Bin, and as a Community Transition Specialist assisting mentally and physically disabled adults for Home Life, Inc. He was also a small press publisher, poetry editor and martial art instructor. Through the Willamette Literary Guild, he coordinated numerous poetry readings, slams and workshops. His favorite venues included Grass Roots Books and Music, The Book Bin, The Interzone, Uncle Hungry's, Corvallis Public Library, Old World Deli and the Corvallis Arts Center. He edited and published several local publications, including Paisley Moon Press's *open unison stop*, *RIVEN* (co-published with Eric Wayne Dickey), *Flight, da Vinci Days*—a poetry anthology (co-edited with Jessica Lamb) and *Tcha teenmanwi: Poems for Marys Peak Anthology* (co-edited with Charles Goodrich). He also served as a poetry editor for *ArtSpirit* and selected poems for the *Midway Marquee*. Michael was part of several poetry groups involving Backer Edition's Sara Backer; Cyrano Press's Jon Munster; Mistry Guild's Candace Poulson and Hollie Messenger; Siski Press's John Ginn; Poets of the Interzone including Ken Day, Chris Gray and Haakon Hofstad; and private workshop groups with Robert Crum, Peter Sears, Steven Sher, Susan Spady and Roger Weaver. He was featured at da Vinci Days festival (OSU), Windfall (Eugene), First Draft (Pendleton), Fishtrap (Joseph), Magic Barrel (Corvallis) and Silverton Poetry Festival. In 2000, he was Writer-in-Residence for Fishtrap. Michael is the author of five poetry books (*blue crow* (LitPot Press), *Mudsong* (Pygmy Forest Press), *Root of Lightning* (Pygmy Forest Press), *Unfolding the Field* (Left Fork) and *dentro do som/inside the sound* (Companhio das Ilhas, Portugal); and a children's book, *Woodwoo—the Little Sasquatch* (Left Fork). His most recent chapbook, *Kahlo's Window* (SurVision Books, Ireland, 2023) won the James Tate Prize. Other poetry awards include the Robert Graves Award, The Turtle Island Poetry Award, runner-up for the Paris Book Festival Award and an honorable mention for the Eric Hoffer Book Award. He has also won a Luso-American Fellowship from DISQUIET International. His poems have appeared in numerous publications including *Atlanta Review, Crannog, Flyway, Gavea-Brown, Midwest Quarterly, New York Quarterly, The Oregonian* and *Spillway*. At the time of his death in late 2024, Michael was a poetry editor for *Pedestal Magazine, Cobra Lily* and Flowstone Press. He lived in Brookings, OR, with his wife Jazmine Blu. His final poems appear in *Approaching Pianowood Harbor* (Flowstone Press, 2025).

Acknowledgments. indecision (*Raintown Review*); the woman Miles Davis turned down (*Sulphur River Literary Review*); beneath a plum tree (*West Wind Review*); fishing with my son (*Hermes Poetry Journal*); what kind of fish can survive this river (Pygmy Forest Press).

indecision

I've walked most of the way
to my car but now

I'm stuck in the middle
of the street watching
a leaf the size of my hand
fall as it holds
an answer for me

my car is full of sun
and the idea
of a room of people
I'll have to greet with
scrap apologies and excuses
as to why I'm late

no doubt I'll be pulled
into a small group of people
and conversation will come to be
jewelry around throats and wrists

it's the suicide of the day
for me to consider anything

more than my friend
behind me in the park
sitting in his shadow
as if it were a boat

I'm interested in his fingers
hooking into the sounds
between brain and guitar

and the simple
act of watching
leaves fall

the woman Miles Davis turned down

she was that bruised
note
he was
looking for:

something to put into his mouth

>   a sound as blue as Sugar
>   Ray Robinson's shadow
>   dance before crushing
>   LaMotta against the ropes

but slow, round
as Jack Johnson's barreling
moan when he met a woman like her

oh, yeah
she was a match for him

and there he was
walking along the edge
of a lake front

thinking of her

>   the taste of her lips
>   before he told her maybe
>   another time
>   he knew what he was doing

she was the jass in jasmine
the last opiate of flesh

the leaves of mullein—
no, the green purr mullein would make
if it were a sound

beneath a plum tree

I play dead
beneath a plum tree
as a breeze begins to bury me
with blossoms

crows in other trees—raucous
and weary—
are not fooled

a dog
shoves its nose against my cheek
bone and licks my face
I almost crack
a smile—I'm not sure
if I can stay dead like this
much longer

I want someone
to touch my shoulders to see
if I move— put an ear
to my chest—shake me!
slap me! jab me in the ribs!

I want someone to gasp—
take hold of my wrists
and pull me out

fishing with my son

      for Max

we're golfing with fishing poles:
from one picnic bench to the other
we cast lures and sinkers
over the glassy park grass

the sky is overcast with occasional
late morning joggers and jogger-nots

and with little surprise we see
a scuffed up soccer ball
in the tall grass

after several sightings all morning
from The Interzone Café rooftop
to the sloughs near the mint field
we're sure this soccer ball followed us
bouncing off bumpers
and windshields as we drove the highway

it is the head from our now headless scarecrow
we thought lost
after punting it into the field

it's eyeballing us for the opportunity to trip us
(and it is tripping us out)

I admit I'm fond of this soccer ball
as it appears when we're not sure
what to say to each other

even though you're my son
we're still getting to know each other

the senseless helps us make sense
of each other

OK, I'll shut up, *soccer ball head*
must be exhausted as it has stopped moving
near the last picnic bench in our course

if we can plunk the head with a sinker
we'll be able to capture it

then when it wakes
it'll be with its body again
stuffed with last year's crumpled news

are you ready?
let's concentrate
and make that one pure cast

what kind of fish can survive this river

that night you told me
you were going to fight in the war
we sat on boulders
overlooking the muddy banks
of the Willamette River

our shoes were battered with muck

the smell of rotting fish
and mildewed rags
settled into itself

a street lamp's light
on the other side floated like a barge
on the slow surface

I didn't want to tell you
I had already dreamed you were a ghost
your spine snapped
from some spinning wing of metal

your chest blown open
and your voice rising with green smoke

frogs and crickets began
to stir the dark
the river moved like a beggar
in a heavy coat

I didn't know what to say
so I brought up old school stories

we joked about what kind of fish
could survive this river

we dreamed up a creature
flat and lumpy
that must convulse to move
eyes on the back of its head
no teeth, no bones

with a mouth on its belly
it sucks contaminated sludge

this made us laugh
and we fell into each other's arms
and hugged for the only time
like brothers

all night I feared
I wouldn't remember your voice

all night I lay in bed and heard
the hiss of cars on asphalt
as planes in the sky

ANN STALEY

Photo courtesy of the poet

In 1970, Ann returned from a two-year stint in the Peace Corps (Brazil). On the summer solstice, she headed west in her VW bug, having never been west of Dayton, OH. She had the address of two retired social workers in Ashland who had gone "back to the land," living in a small cabin with their two small children 19 miles up the Green Springs Highway. They had another small cabin where Ann could stay; she camped out in a tipi that summer. They had an outhouse, no electricity, an organic garden and went into Ashland once a week to do the laundry, shower and make phone calls. Ann applied for a teaching position at Hedrick Junior High School and was hired by a principal who was seeking "diversity." She was the first Ms. in the district of 450 faculty members. She wore Birkenstocks and long skirts, and her purse was a backpack. The following summer, Ann met her husband, Courtney Cloyd, at Twin Plunges. He worked with the US Forest Service. They moved to Gold Beach, Cave Junction, Corvallis and Portland over the next 30 years. When they retired, they moved back to Corvallis. Ann's writing life began in the Willamette Valley. She taught creative writing to adults who didn't want a grade. She loved teaching kids, but the paperwork for a Language Arts Teacher was "a killer": 60-hour weeks. She joined Willamette Valley Writers and formed two poetry groups, Tuesday Writing Group and Saturday Writing Group, and helped Linda Varsell Smith choose poetry contest winners. Ann also taught for 20 years with Kim Stafford at Lewis & Clark College. During this time, she began to think about publishing her work. For years, she thought of herself as a teacher who writes, but when she held her first book, *Primary Sources* (Book Trope Editions, 2011), in her hands, she realized that she had become a writer who teaches. Her other books include *Instructions for the Wishing Light* (Book Trope Editions, 2012); *Confessional Weather* (chapbook, Nota Bene, 2013); *The Age of Bronze* (8th Street Press, 2018); *Willamette Valley—Late March* (Black Cat Press/8th Street Press, 2020); *Fire in the Desert* (8th Street Press, 2020); *Small Beauties* (chapbook, 8th Street Press, 2021); and *The Spirit That Moves in All Things* (8th Street Press, 2021). She was one of the founding editors of *Fireweed*. Ann died in 2022, followed by Courtney within a year.

Acknowledgments. Afternoon Sky, Harney Desert (Black Cat Press); Upwelling (*Primary Sources*); Rhymes with Dammit (*Instructions for the Wishing Light*); November Ghazal (*Primary Sources*); Clouded Nights.

Afternoon Sky, Harney Desert

>from a painting by Frederick Childe Hassam

Highway 20 out of Heppner, driving east, driving south,
cross the county line near the airstrip and the old quarry,
sun glinting in the rearview. *Who lives out here?*
you wonder, and thank god for bottled water.
Drive past the signs for the lakes—Nordell, Sheep, Clusters—
past Moon Reservoir and the Double O Road,
your brother had said. And you do.

Twilight, now, and the lights of Burns
shine like stars you want to get to know.
At the Steens Highway you head south and east again,
like the Union Pacific, like Crane Creek.

At dusk you know you're all alone,
New Princeton deserted decades before the automobile,
and you remember that he'd laughed advising,
No State or County maps will help.

In the darkness you drive with the animal instinct for water,
for the safety of high ground.
Virginia Valley, one-lane, gravel, on somebody's map,
doglegs onto Anderson after about ten minutes of ruts and jolts.
All you hear now is the sound of the car as it moves
through chill air, darkness, snub end of a long day.

You know the desert is out there,
east of the water-soaked Refuge and the Steens.
It's waiting there in Pueblo Valley—white, startling, sands like table salt
despite the Alvord, Indian, Wildhorse, the Sesena, Horse and Willow,
creeks that make it bloom in spring, that have drawn you almost to California.
And where, tomorrow, you will set out your easel and paints—
sky filled with afternoon, desert green-gold with flowering,
the purple Steens, one thin brush-stroke between earth and sky.

Upwelling

Out along Shotpouch, water rilling over rock,
air cool and damp, mud-pathed glory of larkspur,

Late May sunshine arrives,
hazel leaf-shadows dance with the wind.

Star whites emerge among canary grasses,
blackberries barb through cotton gloves,

Bees buzz by the sword fern, distant chain saw,
murmur of voices from the Sacred Cedar Trail.

I say to myself, this day dazzles like no other,
this day obliterates news headlines,

the pain inside a morning kitchen.
Working near the cabin Franz made,

among the thirty thousand trees he planted,
there is only stillness, there is only Now.

Rhymes with Dammit

> *What the river says, that is what I say.*
> William Stafford

The Willamette dares the stranger
to say her name.
One needs the dictionary syllables—
wil am it'—
but even they are confusing.
The river says, "I have a direction,
and although I am racing now
after a January deluge,
I might meander in late August.
I have streamside beds and

the riverbed of the one-hundred-year flood,
a heron's nest at the bridge,
the inevitable otters.
You are welcome here
with your little dramas and sorrows.
You may sit and dream,
or speak to someone
in the Eastern Time Zone,
watch the walkers, the dogs on leashes,
the careening rebel skateboarders.
There is life here, an eternal flow,

one way toward the infinite."

November Ghazal

The only thing I know is the insensible
light disappearing at dusk.

Somehow in the blaze of the fire's flame
I remember my father's hands.

Tell me why a stranger's face on the street
holds my attention, makes me wonder.

Have we all agreed about falling snow,
this white sky dropping is peace on earth?

No one alive now remembers my arrival,
daughter born with eyes open to summer.

It's all right if the melancholy oboe sings all night.
It's all right if geese rest in gray rows of field stubble.

Some Masters say we are all wounded here.
Ann, your wounds are messages from Paradise.

Clouded Nights

    after Edward Steichen

We have them, too,
in the Willamette Valley.
High clouds, a full moon in the distance,
tree and shrub in the foreground.
On nights like this
we sip wine, sit on the back deck
hundreds of white daisies
reflect the moonlight.
Autumn will come, we know,
and then we'll be sitting inside
in front of the fire.

CLEMENS STARCK

Photo courtesy of the poet

Clemens was born in Rochester, NY, in 1937. After dropping out of Princeton, he continued his education on the road, riding freight trains and working at a variety of jobs around the country. He was a ranch hand in eastern Oregon, a newspaper reporter on Wall Street, a door-to-door salesman and a merchant seaman, among other things. For over 20 years he worked construction up and down the West Coast, as a carpenter and carpenter foreman on projects of all kinds, from bridge work in San Francisco and Oregon to custom homes in British Columbia. As a poet he received a scholarship from the Breadloaf Writers Conference as well as a grant and year-long residence at the Helene V. Wurlitzer Foundation of New Mexico. In 1998 he was the Witter Bynner Fellow and poet-in-residence at Willamette University, where he taught on several occasions. In 2004 he was visiting poet at the University of California at Santa Cruz. His poems have appeared in numerous magazines over the years, and in various anthologies. A number of them have been read by Garrison Keillor on National Public Radio and included in Keillor's anthology, *Good Poems for Hard Times* (Viking/Penguin, 2005). He gave readings to diverse audiences in California and throughout the Northwest. A collection of his work, *Journeyman's Wages*, was published by Story Line Press in 1995. The book received the William Stafford Memorial Poetry Award from the Pacific Northwest Booksellers Association, and was also the recipient of the 1996 Oregon Book Award for Poetry. *Studying Russian on Company Time*, an account in verse and prose of his involvement with Russia and the Russian language, appeared in 1999 and was a finalist for the 1999 Oregon Book Award. Another full-length collection of poems, *China Basin*, published in 2002, was also chosen as an Oregon Book Award finalist. Three letterpress chapbooks of poems appeared subsequently: *Traveling Incognito* (2004 and 2007), *Rembrandt, Chainsaw* (2012) and *Old Dogs, New Tricks* (2016). A full compilation of his work, *Cathedrals & Parking Lots: Collected Poems*, was published by Empty Bowl in 2019. He retired in 2004 from his job as a carpenter doing maintenance and repair work at Oregon State University in Corvallis. In spring 2005 he taught a course in postwar central European poetry at Willamette University. Until his death in 2024, he lived on 40-some acres in the foothills of the Coast Range, outside of Dallas, OR. Find out more about Clemens at clemensstarck.com.

Acknowledgments. A Lesson in Physics; Journeyman's Wages; Dismantling; Deciding the Course My Education Should Take; Job No. 75–14. (All these poems appeared in *Journeyman's Wages* and were reprinted in *Cathedrals & Parking Lots: Collected Poems*.)

A Lesson in Physics

One by one the old barns are collapsing.
Just last week one went down
on the Peoria road.
You couldn't say
it was unexpected, racked as it was and leaning
a little more out of plumb
each time I passed.

I'm closing in
on 65 myself. And although
I've been partially rebuilt, with certain adjustments
to my anatomy,
I won't last long.

A new roof and some cross-bracing
would have bought that old barn a few more years.
Triangulation
makes a difference. But in the end, gravity
takes over. Which is why
levity is so precious
while it lasts.

Journeyman's Wages

To the waters of the Willamette I come
in nearly perfect weather,
Monday morning
traffic backed up at the bridge
a bad sign.
            Be on the job at eight,
boots crunching in gravel;
cinch up the tool belt, string out the cords
to where we left off on Friday—
that stack of old
form lumber, that bucket of rusty bolts

and those two beat-up sawhorses
wait patiently for us.

Gil is still drunk, red-eyed, pretending he's not
and threatening to quit;
Gordon is studying the prints.
Slab on grade, tilt-up panels, Glu-lams
and trusses ...

Boys, I've got an idea—
instead of a supermarket
why couldn't this be a cathedral?

Dismantling

    Call Joel (eves) 623-9765

Smack in the public eye
at Ninth and Van Buren, tearing down
an old house—
"Not demolition, dismantling!" says Joel. Slowly
we make the house disappear.
It takes a few months.
We do this for a living.
 Our sign says:
USED LUMBER FOR SALE.
Neat stacks of it on the front lawn
around a dormant forsythia—
shiplap and siding, and over here
we have two-by ...
That pile is already sold.

We also have toilets, sinks, remarkable
savings on bent nails,
French doors, free kindling
and more. Lots more.

...

With the roof off
a house looks more like a cathedral,
rafters outlined against the sky.
A pair of ragged priests,
stick by stick we celebrate
nothing. We are making the shape of nothing,
creating
an absence.

And when we have finished,
what will there be at Ninth and Van Buren?
A square of bare earth
where a house was.
Sidewalk. Foundation. Concrete stoop.
Two steps up
and you're there.

Deciding the Course My Education Should Take

    for Ron

Maybe I already know
as much as I'm destined to know, for this lifetime,
about small-engine repair.
And also about plumbing.
For that matter, I wouldn't mind
drinking a beer
to celebrate
an end to plumbing, and an end to small-engine repair.

Why not study ethno-botany,
or practice juggling?
I could learn to read Chinese, and start in
on the ten thousand poems extant
of Lu You.

It's unlikely I'll take up blacksmithing,
or become a back-hoe operator.

For the time being
I think I'll just concentrate
on finding the words
for the mist that rises from the fields in the morning,
or the moon
as seen once from Joel's truck
on the way home from a job in Corvallis.

Job No. 75-14

    for Ron Boyce

Drive stakes, shoot grades,
get a big Cat to scalp and scrape and gouge:
contour the site for proper drainage.
Berm and swale.

Rough-grade it then, with
a blade, and hope
it don't rain. Set hubs,
haul in base rock, grade it again, then
pave it with a thick crust of blacktop
to make a parking lot.
                      I'm building
a new Safeway, in West Salem,
for some religious millionaire,
and we will all buy our groceries there.

"Well, tomorrow's Friday," I say
to the guy who looks like Jesus driving stakes
and rod-hopping for me,
and he says "Yeah, then two!
and then five and then two and then five …."

Seven being a magic number
and the earth having a thin skin,
we make motions to bow
ceremoniously, but instead, a couple of
unmasked accomplices, confederates
on a losing planet,
we look at each other
and grin—
      which means: "to draw back the lips
so as to show the teeth
as a dog in snarling,
or a person in laughter or pain."

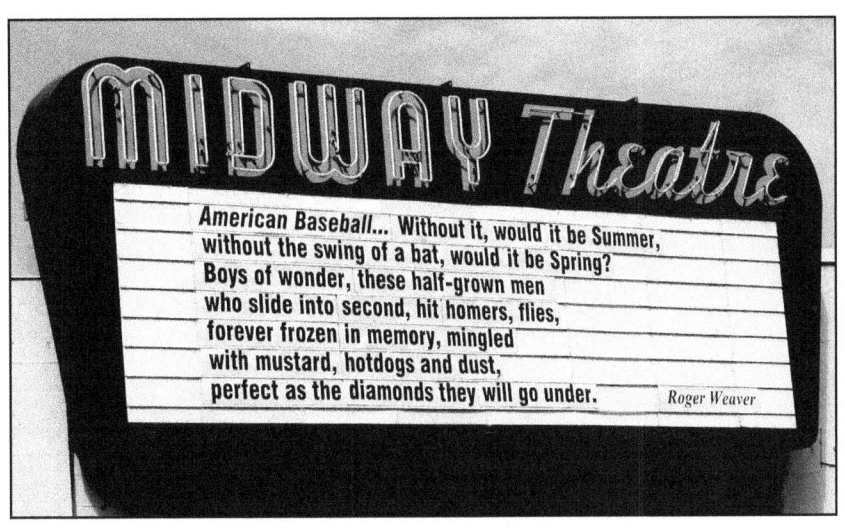

DOUG STONE

Photo courtesy of the poet

Doug, who lives in Albany, OR, has been a social worker, policy analyst and consultant on public policy issues. He has written three poetry collections, *The Season of Distress and Clarity* (Finishing Line Press), *The Moon's Soul Shimmering on the Water* (Clearspace) and *Sitting in Powell's Watching Burnside Dissolve in Rain* (The Poetry Box). He has won the Oregon Poetry Association's Poet's Choice Award and is a Pushcart nominee. His poems have been published in local and regional publications including *Cloudbank, Fault Lines, Fireweed, Willawaw Journal, Timberline Review, Art Spirit* and *The Oregonian*, and in the anthology *A Ritual to Read Together: Poems in Conversation with William Stafford*. Doug has taken poetry writing courses from Roger Weaver and David Biespiel at Oregon State University. He has also participated in several poetry groups in Corvallis over the years, including groups organized by Dale Willey, Linda Smith, Roger Weaver, Michael Malan and Rachel Barton, plus poetry workshops from Peter Sears in Corvallis and Portland. He has read his poetry at several venues in Corvallis and around the Mid-Valley including Grass Roots Bookstore, the Corvallis Public Library, The Interzone Coffee Shop, The Old World Deli, The LaSells Stewart Center at OSU, The Salem Poetry Project and Tsunami Books in Eugene. He has also read in Portland at Powell's Books, the Multnomah County Library, The Lan Su Chinese Garden and at Penelope Scambly Schott's White Dog Salon. Through poetry, Doug tries to come to a better understanding of the Mid-Valley, Oregon and the Northwest.

Acknowledgments. The Wilson River Road (*Sitting in Powell's Watching Burnside Dissolve in Rain*); Spring Arrives in the Hoh Rain Forest (*Cascadia Rising*); Letter from Oregon (*Cascadia Rising*); Requiem for Celilo Falls (*Sitting in Powell's Watching Burnside Dissolve in Rain*); Somewhere between Bend and Boise (*Sitting in Powell's Watching Burnside Dissolve in Rain*).

The Wilson River Road

      thinking of William Stafford

The Wilson River Road can be a nasty stretch of asphalt,
especially at night, shouldering through the mountains
like a mean drunk staggering toward the coast.
But this road is also a poem reciting its way along the river,
its sharp swerves and curves, poetry of pavement reading
the mountain dark. It is a road of shadows, the river's voice,
and South Wind dancing in the trees, a road like life,
so many turns, so many decisions, so many places where
it can all go wrong and midway through your journey,
you may wonder if the trip is really worth it. But as your
headlights search for that final curve near the end of the road,
you feel the ocean breathe new life into your soul.
You're no longer just traveling through the dark.
Now you know you've been on the right road all along.

Spring Arrives in the Hoh Rain Forest

Rain stops.
The slow hands of low clouds open
and shafts of sunlight flash through the understory,
ignite the lush forest a thousand shades of green.
The slow hands of low clouds slip back
over the canopy, turn the forest
a thousand shades of gray.
Rain begins to fall
again.

Letter from Oregon

When I first arrived, I was told I would feel a sadness
in the rain-soaked winter light as if something was lost
and might never be found again. Then I learned to listen
to the rain and walk without the burden of my shadow.
Here the rain tells the truth about everything it touches,
the hard city truth of glistening concrete, glass and steel,
the soft, lush truth of those things green and living,
the quiet truth of a landscape, always under low
slung clouds, flourishing in the song of winter rain.
On those rare days when the winter sun ignites the sky,
it tries to tell me the weight of my shadow is a gift
but I no longer trust the promise of bright, cold light.
Rain will be gray. That is the nature of rain. But it will never
be indifferent and will never lie. That too, is the nature of rain.

Requiem for Celilo Falls

When I was a kid, we used to stop on our way
to my granddad's place in Eastern Washington.
As we walked toward the sound of the falls,
I heard the air shatter, felt the ground quiver.

It was the ancient voices of all those rivers
that make up the Columbia, thrashed to a single
angry roar by the clenched fists of the rocks
then tossed over the falls in a swirling froth
of white water and mist full of leaping salmon.

The roar of the falls is caged in my memory.
I can still hear that anger these many years
after the dams lobotomized those ancient voices
into the placid silence of the Columbia
that can't remember how to be a river anymore.

Somewhere between Bend and Boise

I'm lost in tire song
        on this two-lane blacktop,
                my windshield splattered with stars.

High beams hollow out the dark
        as I power down this unfamiliar road.
                But on this endless, empty highway

there is no danger
        except to die alone
                in wreckage of my own making.

Here, in the middle of nowhere
        I don't need or want a map.
                I'm in this perfect sweet spot

where my future is just
        the road beyond my high beams,
                my past, an empty rear view mirror.

**Poetry
International**

1997

τό τόπος

Poetry
International

2003

pacifica: peace & the sea

ANITA SULLIVAN

Photo by Marcia Mikulak

When Anita came to Corvallis in 1981, Oregon was like a step-mother who immediately offered her a new career, new landscape and new people to fall in love with. As the spinning gradually slowed, she began to earn a living as a piano tuner and discovered the biweekly open poetry workshop at Dale Willey's house, which he and Richard Dankleff—both Oregon State University English faculty—offered to the community. Anita had been writing stories since grammar school, but only in the late '70s did some poems start showing up in her notebooks and in her imagination. She remained in this workshop for the next 10 years, gaining a notion of what it meant to be a poet and holding herself to standards she didn't know were possible for her. Meanwhile, Anita was apprenticing as a piano tuner/technician with Sam Stuart, who had for years been the chief tuner in Corvallis and for OSU. In addition to tuning, rebuilding and repairing old uprights in the garage, they talked about an idea for a book about the philosophy of piano tuning. In 1985, with his help, Anita finished *The Seventh Dragon: The Riddle of Equal Temperament*, published by Metamorphous Press in Portland. It won the 1986 Western States Book Award for creative nonfiction, was reviewed in the *New York Times Book Review* and led to a series of radio broadcasts she did for National Public Radio's *Performance Today*. In the early '90s, Anita focused more on her poetry, publishing a chapbook, *I Hear the Crickets Laughing*, with Howlet Press (1991) in Portland. She offered workshops locally and co-founded the Willamette Literary Guild. She also traveled to Greece four times, wrote a travel essay book and joined another poetry critique group that met at the home of Donna Henderson. In 2000, she met Edwin M. Good, a retired Stanford professor who had authored a well-respected book on the history of the piano. They moved to Eugene together. In 2008, Anita completed an MFA in poetry from Pacific Lutheran University. The same year, Traprock Books in Eugene published her poetry chapbook *The Middle Window*. Her poetry critique group formed itself into a publishing collective, Airlie Press, which published her full-length collection *Garden of Beasts* (2010). Since then, Anita has focused equally on essays and poetry. The most recent essay collection, *The Rhythm of It: Poetry's Hidden Dance* (Shanti Arts Publishing, 2019), is a kind of transfer of the musical principles of tuning a piano to the rhythm patterns underlying "free verse" poetry. It was a finalist for the Eric Hoffer Montaigne Medal in 2021. The most recent poetry book is *Original Flamboyance* (Shanti Arts Publishing, 2022). Find out more about Anita at anitasullivan.org.

Acknowledgments. Wool Light; Willamette-ites (*River Songs*, Willamette River Diptych); Green (*Let us Drink to the River*, reprinted in *A Guide to the Willamette River Water Trail*); Owl Dialogue; The Day Arrives (*Maintenant 14*).

Wool Light

You must know
a certain thing about sheep
my heart constricts
as I approach the task
of pointing out to you
that place where wool just becomes air.

See how the perfect
balance of light-to-wool
is maintained with such
difficulty like the rim
of a volcano,
watch how exactly

they parley: "shall I?"
"would you?" "do you mind?"
not "we," or bliss.
The light is always leaving as if leaving
were coming home.

Willamette-ites

We face the river, our faces
are rubbed by river
as if we were the moon, or maybe
someone backing out of a room at gunpoint.
Our round faces, polished daily by waterish light,
our souls too, perhaps are river color, purled
drowned, fish-infested, browned in
river's dirt, embraced by its sly
elbows and high muckety-muck
personhood. Our umbilical selves swell
always in the direction of its water, our doom
turns ever upon its familiar belly-shine.

Green

Nineteen shadows, filterings
   leanings of leaf, overlappings, angles
   dapplings and precise penetrations of late
        afternoon sun
along this old river slough
cause the nineteen species of grass
   bush, tree, lily, sedge
   rush and weed to glow
with a thousand different hues,
my shirt, too, the brand new cedar fence posts,
and the gate that rests without hinges
between barbed wire and tree.
Where will it end, this one color
made into a sphere of everything we need?
My toes rejoice among the lower grasses.

A black and white osprey hunts
   along the slough
but his heart is green.

Owl Dialogue

In the summer of the first Plague Year, gardeners
began to notice certain shadows in early afternoon,

shadows that rippled across the spade-like leaves of giant
sunflowers—but nothing overhead, not even clouds.

"Owls," said one old timer, squinting upwards as if
a stovepipe connected her directly to the nearest patch of sky.

"Nothing else has wings that dense and goes so low
to the ground," she nodded. "Owls."

But where are they, these daylight owls?
"Invisible," the old timer said. She frowned.

"Worlds overlapping here, mixing illusions. Not good,
high risk of contamination."

"Could be an omen, too, one foot in each camp you might say.
Keep an eye on it—if it spreads to the nightshades is when I'd

start digging the shelter; cept'n the soil's so cracked
and hard as cement these days."

"Some cracks already deep enough to hide a truck in," quipped someone
with a quiet voice, and after that the conversation fizzled

and the shadows of invisible owls were assumed into our second world
as if they had always belonged.

The Day Arrives

Yesterday, that meadow along the highway
was safely horizontal—
a short, fat meadow gleaming greenly
behind a managed forest of anorexic alders,
meadow with a belly on it, jolly
but docile.

Today that meadow seems preoccupied;
it rises, almost vertical behind the trees,
flapping lightly, exposing stretch marks, stains,
crushed-nap smudges. Rabidly
it sops up the morning's yellow luminosity
like a toast set loose among the eggs.

The anemic, gracile alders
are beginning to bend,
almost to squint, or turn their trunks around
like owls
in a collective quake of anticipation.
What day is this?

Their roots have been bound for so long,
assuming they remember
the terms of the original agreement,
they still may stumble while they're walking out.

PEGGY TAYLOR

Photo from How Sweet the Sound *by permission of
University of Oregon Knight Library Special Collections*

Peggy lived in Corvallis with her husband, Dave, and her blue-heeler dog, Star. A graduate of Oregon State University, she loved the outdoors with a passion. Her favorite pastime was walking in the woods and wilderness, backpacking and exploring backroads. Her poems reflect her close connection with the natural world, her curiosity, her courage and humility as well as her humor. They also reflect her love of mythology (especially English/Irish). Her book of poetry *How Sweet the Sound* was published in 1999 (Type-Ink, Corvallis) shortly before her death, with editing contributions, advice and support from members of the Corvallis writing community. Peggy had been fighting breast cancer since 1990 and felt that if she was going to print her poetry, then it had better be sooner than later. The book was published with generous donations from the Rebekahs, Oregon State University Center for Humanities and private individuals in the community. It was, she said, "quite an experience—like turning over the baby to a new babysitter." Her poetry appeared in many local publications such as *CALYX Journal, The Eloquent Umbrella* and *Prism*.

Acknowledgments. Fairie Tail; Brigid (*CALYX Journal*); Walking the Dog; I Can …; To My Lover's Legs. (All these poems appeared in *How Sweet the Sound* and were selected by Anita Sullivan.)

Fairie Tail

Lower the bucket into the well
and see what comes up perched
on the wet wooden edge,
frog-eyes, splayed-toes, toad-grin.
Skin splits to release wings
to glisten above the damp back.
The beast winks at you familiarly,
leaps from the bucket to ground,
and hops down the dusty road.
With each leap
pebbles change to pearls,
dust to down, the weeds to jasmine.
And still change spreads
until the world glistens
and is born again, borne
from warted back and wing-dust,
dewed and cleansed in the water
of the well.

Brigid

The Brigid, Irish earth mother, brews
the beer that is time, fermentation
to the fall of sand, birth of a star.
She draws water from a black pool of no tide
where stars swim in the midnight
and, with a kiss, blesses the new.

And beer brews and yeast bubbles,
and the world spins in the dark Milky Way.

On limestone cliffs the Brigid stands
high above the waves, feet planted, cornsilk hair
alive with visions of animals:
of deer, bear and cows,
of cranes and swallows,

of mice, salamanders and snakes.
She hears whale song upon the waves,
long and low, a paean that echoes
in the fluid cathedral, leaves the woman, the
world ringing, ringed in song and sound.

And still the Brigid brews,
aged dugs asway in rushlight,
gold hair of youth in firelight.

Body stained dark as beer, heart rich
as the land, she moves in rhythm with Earth,
sings with the beat of time, bends with pain,
births with each batch a new age of the world.

Walking the Dog

Sirius, the dog star, heels at Orion's ankle,
muzzle turned to the Rabbit, Lepus.
My whistle into the night is only a puff of breath;
the dog comes anyway, eyes green phosphorescence
in the streetlight, tongue wet on my fingers.

I throw the frisbee, slimy with saliva,
across the face of Mars: a red eye
like a wolf at the edge of a campfire.
The dog returns, shaking the toy
as if it were a rat, lays it at my feet,
then backs off, ears pricked in expectation.
I can feel his urgency, a plea in the air
as palpable as the steam of breath.

I throw again and his galloping feet recede
into the warble and shimmer of frog song
at the edge of the swamp,
the persistent procreational cry.
Returning, the dog stops by a tree, sniffs,
urinates, hot liquid hissing against the rough bark.

I whistle, he procrastinates. I call, clap my hands.
Finally, in his own time, he returns, frisbee-less.
I send him back with an order to "Find."
The rim of a ten o'clock moon appears
over Snow Mountain. I watch the dog
snuffle in the long grass at the field's edge
as the moon inflates out of the earth like a balloon,
a clown face, lacking only a cherry nose.

The dog comes to lie at my feet, mouth open,
breath hot on my leg. Turning back, I see
the light of my front porch, the television
flickering blue behind the curtains.
As the moon spreads a sheet across the stars,
I follow my shadow back over the grass to warmth,
the dog, replete with running, at my heel.

I Can ...

Run my hand along
the flanks of the ridge,
stroke the live flesh beneath,
feel the fur of the trees
rustle against my palm,
prick between my fingers ...

Hold the moon in my lap, let its light
merge and mingle with my flesh,
tingle its way into my veins,
roll its mystery around
the chambers of my heart ...

Open my skull from ear to ear
so the wind sweeps out the *secret places*
then swirls the dust away
on bellowing breath
to leave my brain shining
like polished marble ...

Sleep in the salt sea
surrounded by its body,
flesh within flesh,
blood within blood,
cradled in the warmth of its arms.
Where all my little deaths
of fear, pain and guilt
wash away, carried by the same
currents that bring life.

To My Lover's Legs

His legs are hairy,
short and heavy,
elemental muscle and bone,
veined, knobby at the knees.

His legs have carried him
over mountains, up ridges slick
with scree, down trails,
through glacier-fed creeks.

His legs climbing before me bunch
with muscle, dirt dotting each pore,
tendons behind the knee stand out,
sharp and taut as rope.

His legs have been burned by the sun,
roughened by dust and rock
until their skin and hair rasps
beneath my fingers.

But at rest, his legs are furred,
covered with a soft pelt
fine as an otter's coat,
as they rub between mine.

ROGER WEAVER

Photo courtesy of the poet

A native Oregonian, Roger was born in Portland and moved with his family to the mid-Willamette Valley as a child. His poetry is both a product and portrayal of Oregon. A graduate of North Salem High School, the University of Oregon and the University of Washington, he has published six books and over 70 poems in poetry journals. His books are *The Orange and Other Poems* (Press-22, 1978), *Twenty-One Waking Dreams* (Trout Creek Press, 1985), *Traveling on the Great Wheel* (Gardyloo Press, 1990), *Reading the Stones: New and Selected Poems* (Poetry Enterprises, 2003) and *The Ladder of Desire* (Pygmy Forest Press, 2006). Journal publications include *The North American Review, The Dog Review, Hubbub, Massachusetts Review, The Greenfield Review, Nimrod* and *Manzanita Quarterly*. His poetry has been set to music and presented at choral concerts. Roger led poetry writing workshops as an Oregon State University professor and throughout the Northwest, attracting local writers, national scholars, Oregon State University football players and students to the craft of poetry. He held weekly workshops at his home and helped a wide diversity of writers craft their poems. He also edited *To Topos*, a journal dedicated to giving voice to poets worldwide who had no forum for their poetry. His latest work, *The Shape of the Wind* (52 new poems, 2018), reflects how Roger converted his observations of nature into the personal as he added feeling to what is observed. He found the openness of people to listen and go to poetry events in Corvallis at the end of the 20th century inspiring, and loved the collegiality among local poets. Roger died in 2023.

Acknowledgments. Build Down; What the Azaleas Didn't Say; Patterns; Fir Trees; Skating up the Sky (with original drawing by the poet). (All these poems appeared in *The Shape of the Wind*.)

Build Down

The beauty of simplicity
is building down the one
true thing you cannot live
without. It will find you,
swift as a leaf-stripping wind,
silent as the hinges
on the door of sleep
and as the bird's wing
sculpts the wind.

What the Azaleas Didn't Say

The price of passion; its intensity.
The expense of brevity.
The cost of being rooted,
Never being able to walk away.

Patterns

Sun shadows sweep
my windows, land on
the carpets spilling
bright gules, red and blue;
What falls to ground
teaches me to pay
attention ... Patterns
 wait to be discovered.

Fir Trees

Where fir trees herringbone
up a mountain, hope rises,
in the season when musty
mushrooms bloom and spore,
tantalizing the tongue so it may
dazzle us with galaxies
of words rising like fir
branches a bristle in countless
leaves. Stop awhile. Lean
against the trunk.
Be a friendly brother.

Skating up the Sky

Skating up the sky
heart goes, high above
cockcrow, wren wing,
hawk cry.

DALE WILLEY

Photo courtesy of Dave Willey

Dale was a professor of English at Oregon State University whose influence on the Corvallis poetry scene was legendary. He led a long-running poetry workshop at his home that many of the local poets attended. His collection of poems, *Tin Box Papers, and Other Poems* (Oregon Sunrise Press, 2001), appeared the same year that he died. In this book, Dale excerpted passages from letters and a bound journal that were found after the 1963 Christmas floods by a trout fisherman in a tin box wrapped in a waterproof cloth in a corner of a half-destroyed fireplace. The cabin that sat on a shelf above the Rogue River had been washed away. All that stood was the chimney. Dave Willey, Dale's son, is a multi-instrumentalist and composer who has been very active in avant-garde rock since breaking onto the scene in the '90s with Hamster Theatre. His album *Immeasurable Currents* (Dave Willey & Friends, 2011) is an homage to his father. The 12 songs were composed of lyrics from Dale's book *Tin Box Papers*. Dale and his wife Brent (who died in 2010) were active in the Corvallis Unitarian Universalist Fellowship and focused considerable energies on issues of social justice and environmental conservation.

Acknowledgments. Ionesco's Theme; I Could Eat You Up; The Old Woods; Nightfall; The Sinuous. (All these poems appeared in *Tin Box Papers, and Other Poems;* all but "The Sinuous" also appeared on the album *Immeasurable Currents.*)

Ionesco's Theme

> *Our eyes have grown tired from so much light.*
> Eugene Ionesco, *Present Past Past Present*

At the touch of wind the aspen leaves tremble.
Our eyes, grown tired from so much light,
turn inward to rooms washed with mirrors

whose re-collected light never trembles;
we are confirmed in the wash of mirrors
and rest our eyes tired from so much light.

Images kept pure in the wash of mirrors
will never ask us for such light
that moved like aspen leaves we tremble.

Because our eyes are tired from so much light,
in these rooms sunlight bathes no mirror.
Only dappled under aspen trees it trembles.

Our lives are deep in rooms washed with mirrors,
a redundancy secure, while aspens tremble.
Our eyes have grown tired from so much light.

Though at touch of wind the aspen leaves tremble,
our eyes have grown tired from so much light.
We turn inward to rooms washed with mirrors,
cherish here these images, this light.

I Could Eat You Up

> *"And into ashes all my lust"*
> Andrew Marvell, "To His Coy Mistress"

Hans is back at the ruined hut.
Gretel's off to sing in Bremen.
(She has a voice, a handsome woman;
She just adores her Hansel but

Incest's forbidden. She's on the run.)
He picks some gem up out of the ashes.
It smells of dead enchantments. Trash is
Everywhere. The cage is open.

The oven's shut; what's inside
He quakes to think. Behind that rust
Ten years of hate have turned to dust
To cling to him like a ruddy bride.

She may get him yet. Witch-blind,
Whether finger or bone she couldn't know.
But she couldn't wait for it to grow;
Gretel took over. She's still behind

The door. His courage up, he pries;
His stick cracks through iron.
A bit the worse for age and firing,
The witch looks out with no surprise.

Now here is Hans in the suburbs. He drinks
His beer with the guys. The witch is
Cooking up kraut in the kitchen.
Gretchen's quite a little gal, he thinks.

The Old Woods

> *These are the old woods, miasmas, and deers.*
> a note on a painting of a Tibetan forest by An Xu

If it were merely fog, say,
and the boles rose
through it into sun,
if through deep shadows
the slanting light
caught the deer
in a haze drifted in
from elsewhere,
maybe we could bear it.
These old woods
might be safe yet.
But these deer
and those to come
stand and will go
in such fumes as rise
from oil-soaked
matter in a sodden floor.
Miasmas are taking
the old woods, these deer,
and more.

How can we tell
what's human
when these woods
are gone?

Nightfall

        Harney County, Oregon

quail
        one
                then one
                        then one
                              sidelit

hollows deepen
        crickets' rhythm slows
above in sunlight
        nighthawks veer
blue thunderheads butt the west hill
from the mesa oozes the broad moon
        it leaps (coyote call there
                        and there
                                  there)
        rises into the stars
the high desert lies open
        white

The Sinuous

Perhaps the nude
has just emerged
from the serpent
which now lies
along her thigh
limp and spent
or perhaps the serpent
has just sloughed
its skin bends
it head beside
the nude's impassive face
stares into its own eyes

how the snake's body
follows and counters
the nude's curves

the intimacy of curves
the road hugs the hill's rhythm
the car writhes
with the yellow stripe
sways as the hill sways
beyond this hill
on either side
other hills
rise and fall
in serpentine undulations

the
eloquent umbrella

Linn-Benton Community College
Journal for the Creative Arts

THE ELOQUENT UMBRELLA

A Journal for the Creative Arts
1998

Cloudbank Books announces a reading by
Lex Runciman and George Estreich
from their new books
May 27 at 7:30 pm
Corvallis-Benton County Library

Textbook Illustrations of the
Human Body by George Estreich
Winner of the Rhea and Seymour Gorsline
Poetry Prize 2003

Out of Town
by Lex Runciman
Third book in the Northwest Poetry Series

Sponsored by
Grass Roots Books & Music

Valley Writers Series
1991 - 1992

Wednesday, February 26
LBCC, Forum-104, Noon-1 p.m.
Steven Sher
Writer, educator, and editor, Steven Sher has published six books, including poetry and short fiction, with three new manuscripts at press. With an MFA in creative writing, an MA in journalism/mass communications, and a BA in sociology, Sher brings a diverse background to his work. Interested in the writer's visionary qualities, Sher believes that poets can help rescue the contemporary world from its malaise and misdirection.

Wednesday, March 4
LBCC, Forum-104, Noon-1 p.m.
C.K. Williams
C.K. Williams lives in Paris and teaches at George Mason University in Virginia. In 1987, Farrar, Straus and Giroux published his poetry collection, *Flesh and Blood*, which won the National Book Critics' Circle Award for poetry. Williams is the author of four volumes of poetry: *Lies*, *I Am the Bitter Name*, *With Ignorance*, *Tar*, and a collection titled *C.K. Williams: Poems 1963-1983*. He also has published three works of translation.

Thursday, April 23
Corvallis-Benton County Library, 7 p.m.
Friday, April 24
LBCC, Forum-104, Noon-1 p.m.
Susan Landgraf
Teaching writing and journalism at Highline Community College since 1986, Susan Landgraf serves as advisor for the college's newspaper, the *Thunderword*, published bi-weekly. With an MFA in creative writing and a BA in English, Landgraf has pursued her interests in anthropology at the University of Washington, exploring myth, stories and legends to discover how they reveal and shape individuals and cultures. She is widely published as a poet, fiction writer, reviewer, and photographer.

Wednesday, May 6
LBCC, Forum-104, Noon-1 p.m.
Elizabeth Beverly
A poet, playwright, and ethnographer, Elizabeth Beverly writes for and works with children and adults. She teaches through the Northwest Writing Institute at Lewis and Clark College in Portland.

Wednesday, May 13
LBCC, Forum-104, Noon-1 p.m.
Open Mike
Local writers and poets are encouraged to attend and read their works. Contributors to the *Eloquent Umbrella*, LBCC's literary magazine, will share their submissions. If you, or someone you know is interested in reading as part of the Open Mike program, simply attend this event or call Linda Smith or Jane White at 928-2361, ext. 219.

Wednesday, May 20
LBCC, Forum-104, Noon-1 p.m.
Corvallis-Benton County Library, 7 p.m.
Richard Moeschl
As a free lance writer, Richard Moeschl serves as director of Star Resources with the aim of making the wonders of the sky accessible. He writes the weekly column "Exploring the Sky" for a regional magazine and has published a book by the same name. Moeschl writes, directs, and hosts weekly astronomy shows on both public radio and public television. Active as an educator in the Elderhostel program for the past three years, Moeschl has taught in Scotland and in many areas of the United States. His background includes a BA in art and education from Goddard College, Vermont, and a teaching certificate from Emerson College in England.

Linn-Benton Community College
6500 Pacific Blvd. SW
Albany, Oregon 97321

Sponsored by Corvallis-Benton County Library, LBCC's English Department, LBCC's Albany Center & the Associated Students of LBCC

www.ingramcontent.com/pod-product-compliance
Lightning Source LLC
Chambersburg PA
CBHW061757070526
44586CB00023B/2613